AF576795

KEYS TO SUCCESSFUL DATING

(Dating Dynamics)

Keys to

SUCCESSFUL DATING

(Dating Dynamics)

by

JOHN D. HAWKES

Published by

HAWKES PUBLICATIONS
156 W. 2170 S. (Box 15711)
Salt Lake City, Utah 84115
In Utah Call: 487-1695
Toll Free: (1) (800) 453-4616

Copyright 1973

by Hawkes Publications

Library of Congress Catalog Card No. 73—79492

First Printing, June, 1973

Printing—Binding—Distributing

By

HAWKES PUBLICATIONS

DEDICATION

Dedicated to your personal success in dating.

—AUTHOR'S NOTE—

The author feels great reluctance in presenting personal experiences lest they be misunderstood. He hopes the readers will realize that when he does submit to the approach of personal experiences, that they are NOT emotional traumas to the author, and that they are given merely as a testimonial, as a case-in-point to illustrate the reality of feelings and thoughts that do exist in others. From long hours of counseling and visiting with friends he knows that his own experiences presented in this book are common to many others.

The author wishes to thank all of those persons who have contributed to the preparation of this work, including those in the production plant, whose efforts have made this book possible.

TABLE OF CONTENTS

WHAT IS THIS BOOK ABOUT?

Have you ever scanned the libraries for a book on dating that would be helpful in actual dating situations? The books can usually be broken down into three categories:
(1) Religious books pleading the cause of morality.
(2) Psychology books reporting research on sex behavior.
(3) Degenerate books promoting new morality and free love.
The few books which really do get into the dating situations treat the subject in an adolescent manner and are written by married individuals who have forgotten what it is really like.

WRITTEN BY A SINGLE PERSON: Your author was single during the writing of this book, with 17 years of dating experience behind him. "Is that something to brag about," you ask? "You are obviously incompetent and a failure! What is your problem??" The author is not bragging. Yes, he's had his share of failures and disappointments and has experienced the usual problems that others have. He would suggest that his failures have taught him more than his successes. Your author is convinced that his single state has permitted him to perceive and analyze the dating world in far greater depth than any married person could.

While obtaining a B.S. in Psychology and an M.A. in Religion, this author took pains to take clippings and notes from a great deal of reading material that applied to the subject. While teaching University students he researched the problems through lengthy questionnaires and interviews. He prepared questionnaires for young marrieds about their feelings, about their previous dating experiences and their related problems in marriage. He directed many study groups with friends that were both married and single to determine their feelings about many of the more perplexing areas of the dating world. For many years the author has kept diary-like notes of his dating experiences, his successes and his failures. He has written at length his feelings of joy and frustration--lest he forget.

This volume is addressed to both men and women, with the belief that each will understand their own positions better if they are able to perceive the challenges that their partners face. Your author feels that of all the areas of human interaction--there are none so sacred and sublime as the interactions that take place between two young people as they intertwine their hearts and emotions with each other. It is exciting and *DYNAMIC!* Thus the subtitle of this book: *Dating Dynamics.*

GENERAL TOPICS COVERED IN THE CHAPTERS: (1) How do I get a date? (2) Where to go on a date. (3) Deepening the relationship. (4) How do you know when you should get married? (5) What is love? (6) Falling out of love. (7) Why be moral? (8) What is the opposite sex looking for? (9) Developing a dating personality!

GOAL OF THE BOOK: The goal of this book is to create a guide for the dating world that daters can turn to for answers to many questions, and instill a philosophy that will answer the remaining questions. The subject is highly controversial and everyone will have a different opinion. The author does not seek the readers' total agreement. He merely hopes to stimulate the kind of thought that will help dating people to find their own keys to successful dating.

Chapter 1

HOW DO I GET A DATE?

WHERE DO I START? How can I become more datable? Where can I go to meet potential dates? What should I say when I ask a person for a date? How do others approach the situation, what's proper? What does the opposite sex expect and what do they like or dislike? These and many other questions are asked by all of us who want to become more successful in our dating.

DEVELOP A DATING ATTITUDE!

Successful dating begins with our attitudes! In the second chapter we will talk about many of the mechanical steps of dating--but all of these steps put together are not nearly as important to us as our basic attitude towards ourselves and those we date.

How often have you heard something like the following: "I'd like to double date with you, Ed, but I can't get a date." If there is a girl present, a statement like that would make her blow up and reply: "All you have to do is go and ask someone, stupid! You fellows don't know how good you have it!"

The young lady doesn't really understand what the fellow is saying, nor does she realize that it is often more complex than it appears from her position. What Bill is really saying is: "I don't want to just ask any girl. All of the girls I would like to date have turned me down or are busy. And besides, I don't want to date just for dating's sake, I'm tired of it."

Well, anyone could take Bill's argument and tear it to pieces. Everyone would like to give Bill some sound advice and they usually do! They are sure that Bill has a poor attitude.

PROBLEM 1: "SHOULD I DATE WHEN I'M NOT REALLY INTERESTED IN DATING?"

We often find ourselves in Bill's position. The ones that we want to ask or be asked by are not available. We decide that we are tired of the dating game and refuse to ask or be asked unless it is someone that we are really interested in. We want to feel something extra special for the person. But there are several things wrong with just waiting for the big "romantic crushes!" A few of the reasons are as follows:

1. We will probably wait long periods in between dates. I have had friends that have followed this philosophy and haven't got around to dating for many months and even years. It is highly unlikely that you will find your mate if you don't keep looking and you'll never marry someone you don't date!
2. One of the best places to meet other potential dates is on dates. If we are waiting for the romantic storm to hit, it will probably hit less often when we take ourselves out of circulation. We look more attractive in the company of others than we do alone.
3. If we are not dating regularly when a romantic bomb hits, we will probably be awkward and unnatural because we will be out of practice in dealing with dating situations.
4. The whole approach is backwards. There may be some love at first sight, but it often melts on second sight. The romances that last usually come by route of developing a relationship over a period of time. So many marriages come from situations where the couples had no intentions of getting serious at first.
5. Individuals that keep themselves all couped up waiting for their "knight in shining armor" or their beauty queen to break through their dark walls and find them will only make themselves more miserable.

6. Those who remain home, saying they don't wish to waste their time, are often guilty of a selfish element in their personality. Is it a waste of time to interact with other human beings? Is it a waste of time to make friends and try and take an interest in someone else? They may not turn out to be permanent friends, but this in no way voids the worth-while moments we spend with others. One of the greatest needs in the world is more people that "like people" and can simply enjoy being with people, taking an interest in them, listening to them and helping them feel worth-while. If we lose ourselves in others, we shall find ourselves and maybe even that "special person" as well. If we are not "people oriented," then we should try and develop that quality in our personality. We will not only be happier, but we will be amazed at what a difference it can make in our dating success. So, DATE, even if it is just for dating's sake. When we stay in circulation we learn more about dealing with people. We become more outgoing, more generous and warm up our entire personality. If we are to catch a fish we must go fishing! Therefore we should work to apply rule or **KEY 1: STAY IN CIRCULATION!!**

PROBLEM 2: "SHOULDN'T I WAIT UNTIL I AM SURE I HAVE FOUND SOMEONE THAT MEETS MOST OF MY REQUIREMENTS FOR A MATE?"

The next thing they will lecture poor Bill on is that he is too picky. You aren't going to find a perfect girl; you're not perfect so how can you expect others to be? The glamour of the hollywood movies, the fictitious nature of novels and other elements of our society combine to give us unrealistic dreams. We resent being told that we expect too much, but down deep we know that it might be true at times. What kinds of expectations are right, when are we expecting and demanding too little or too much? What is it we really want from dating? The following are ten expectations that many of us have. Notice how they limit our dating scope as they progress downward. We could probably date most people if our expectation list only included the first few.

GENERAL EXPECTATIONS:

1. We want someone to do things with, we want companionship.
2. We want someone to give us friendship, to understand and accept us.
3. We want someone that meets our ideals, moral standards and religious beliefs.
4. We want someone that has a pleasing personality, one who is kind and considerate.
5. We want someone that we feel is good-looking, impressive, intelligent, someone we can be proud to be with.
6. We want someone that we can trust and depend upon to fulfill our needs. We want someone that will provide for us, protect us, and take care of us.
7. We want someone that we can in some measure call our own; we want to possess and be possessed. This is "my girl" or "my fellow."
8. We want someone that we are romantically in love with and who will love us in return.
9. We want someone to provide and create a home atmosphere.
10. We want someone that we feel we could marry and spend a lifetime with and longer.
    (In addition to these general areas we each have our own little areas we hope for.)

We should have high expectation levels! But we should not expect to have all our dreams fulfilled in the first date. We can't start off with everything. We really shouldn't place very many expectations or requirements in order to have a first date with a person. Intellectually we understand all of this, but the emotional portion of us still tends to look for more than we should! Realizing this we should try to overrule our emotional drive by intellectually asserting that we will minimize our expectation level. We should be less rigid in demanding so much of others before we consider them for a simple "first date"!

JUSTIFIED DEMANDS. Yes, there are certain things we cannot tolerate. If the person is crude and offensive in their manner, we should not date them. If our particular beliefs in God are very special and sacred to us, we must have someone that will not only respect us for those convictions, but will share them with us! If we have a college degree and think on a more intellectual plane, it would be ridiculous to date someone that appears to have the intelligence of a grade school child. There are all kinds of levels: social, intellectual, religious, etc., that must be taken into account. We don't have to know very much about some people to realize that there would be absolutely no common grounds on which to develop a relationship. However, assuming that we are going to places where people do think and act on a similar level or plane, we should be able to find many individuals that could pass the basics and qualify for a first date.

If we can just *lessen some of the secondary expectations,* we can open up so many more possibilities and be more successful with those we are already dating. It is hard to forget about looks, but try to place more stress on the personality. Date personalities! To increase our possibilities then, we may apply **KEY 2: LESS RIGIDITY IN OUR DEMANDS!**

PROBLEM 3: "SHOULD I DATE SOMEONE IF I DON'T FEEL ANY ROMANTIC EXCITEMENT TOWARD THEM?"

ROMANTIC INCLINATION: Usually placed above all the other factors which determine who it is that we date is that romantic inclination. It is hard to stay away from those that you are romantically excited about and it is difficult to date those where it is lacking. The individual may not qualify for any of our basic and justified requirements--but we still desire to be with them. If someone asks us why we want to go with them so badly--we really don't know. *THE PERSON INTRIGUES US: THEY MAKE US CURIOUS TO KNOW MORE ABOUT THEM.* There is something *different* about them we like. If we try to intellectualize the reasons, we usually end up telling them that we like the way they smile or the way they hold their head or just the way they look at us. Big intellectual reasons? No. All we know is that there is something mysterious and magical about it all. We recognize the exciting feeling, but we can't explain it very well.

Even before we meet these individuals we will often endow them with the virtues of the gods. They are kind, considerate, accepting, alive, fun, intelligent, etc. We couldn't be happier until we finally get the message that they have absolutely no interest in us. Then we declare: How could they be so thoughtless and cruel? Why don't they at least give us a chance? We become very depressed and our minds become an instant TV replay of all our previous failures. We feel we shall never meet anyone special. And we feel as one of my friends once said to me: "Anyone that would have me couldn't be worth having!" Does that describe how we feel at times?

It's always the same old story with boy and girl. We are so often interested in those that aren't interested in us. The whole dating experience becomes very threatening, emotional and depressing. To be successful and happy in dating we must *take ourselves less seriously,* as well as those we date. We must create an atmosphere of fun and lightheartedness. We need to date those we know better and we will be less likely to be disappointed because of them. Instead of setting out with the purpose in mind of getting serious, we should set out to keep it Platonic and to have fun--you might say, "play-tonic." Then keep it that way until we have time to build a foundation in our relationship that can handle romance.

The following is an experience which happened to the author: While attending college one year, I attended the same church group actively for the entire year. I was sure that I had given every girl there the "total analysis" for dating. At the end of the school year, after finals and after many had already left the campus town for home, a group of the fellows decided to have a canyon cook-out with dates. Since so many had already left town, I didn't know who to ask. Finally a girl in this church group was recommended. I reluctantly agreed to ask her. It turned out to be an exciting date! She looked so cute I couldn't understand how I hadn't noticed her before in all the times I had been around her. Well, this is just one of so many experiences I have had since. Once I have actually placed myself in a dating situation with a person, I have so often found them just the opposite of what I had anticipated. Even when you think you know a person well, you learn a lot more about them once you become "courageous" enough to date them.

What do experiences like these teach us? They support all three of our first rules or keys: 1. *Stay in circulation*--it pays off. 2. *Lower the threshold of our initial demands,* and we may discover a lot of wonderful people to date. 3. *Date for fun*--and the romance we are really hoping for may jump out at us. We should be more willing to date the "average types" around us that don't necessarily set us on fire at first thought.

If we can keep a more "play-tonic" attitude towards most of our dating, we will be less likely to be subjecting ourselves to the disappointments and emotional miseries that accompany so much dating where we are chasing the romantic rainbows. We will be more happy and successful in dating if we attempt to apply the **THIRD KEY: DEVELOP A "PLAY-TONIC" ATTITUDE!**

PROBLEM 4: "IT'S SO HARD TO GET A DATE, WHERE CAN I GO TO FIND DATES?"

DATES FOR STUDENTS. The most natural place to find potential dates is at school. If you are younger, it would be the public schools. If you are of college age, then you will find plenty of potential dates around a college campus. If there is a paradise for daters, it is the college campus! There are many that go on to college just for the purpose of meeting a companion. Some college campuses are better for social life than others. Small town campuses usually have more activities and the students become more involved in school life than in a large city where most students live at home and commute to school. Some of the places to find potential dates in schools would be as follows:

1. *CLASSES.* Classrooms alone can be great places to meet potential dates. Some majors are better than others for putting you in company with the opposite sex. If you are in Elementary

Education, most of your classes will have very few fellows. This should not determine your major, but it might be a consideration. Smaller classes are usually more congenial than massive television classes. Dancing classes would probably be first on the list, because you have a chance to meet, talk with, and actually hold each other!

There are a number of other classes that would also give you some direct social contacts: sports i.e., tennis, archery, golf, etc.; some science labs which are informal and will often have some field trips at times; courtship and marriage classes which are excellent; speech, debate and drama classes, music classes, art classes, etc. There are certainly many fields that you could become interested in which would have good social situations for meeting potential dates. Whether you are working toward a degree or not, you can still enroll for a few classes. And while you are in the classes, go out of your way to meet people!

2. *SOCIAL ACTIVITIES.* Join school organizations, clubs, social units, service organizations. Go to all of the major sporting events. Get involved in student government.

3. *CHURCH GROUPS.* There are usually some excellent church groups at every university. Take some religious classes, since these are most excellent in placing you in the company of individuals that think and feel as you do about the religious realm and who share the same values. Could there be a more ideal place to meet a partner you plan to trust and devote your life to, than to meet them in a religious setting?

DATES FOR NON-STUDENTS. If you cannot involve yourself in a campus life even on a limited basis, then there are still many places you can go to meet potential dates:

1. *SERVICES.* Become active in some civic organizations, some service movements. Investigate the Red Cross volunteers, the Community Action centers, youth camps, etc.

2. *POLITICS.* Become active in politics, find a candidate you feel good about and get involved with others.

3. *SPORTS.* One of the best ways to meet people is through some medium of sports. Don't allow any self-

consciousness to hold you back. If you feel you are just too weak in sports to dive into something, take a few lessons and gain the confidence. The classes are some of the greatest places to meet potential dates. You might challenge yourself to take on several new sports that you have never tried. Every sport has its advantages and some are better than others for meeting people. Skiing is becoming more popular and socially oriented all the time. Tennis is not expensive and doesn't take very long to learn, and you can meet people at larger court areas. Golf can be a social sport depending on where you go to play. Many areas have excellent beaches or swimming pools. There are endless clubs you can join in connection with many sports, such as bowling, horseback riding, sailing and flying clubs, and exploration and adventure clubs.

4. *DANCING.* Then we come back to dancing. There are always classes being offered in every city and stag dances are held to help people mix more. Dancing seems to have been invented for singles to meet singles. It is one of the most natural situations to meet potential dates. Dancing skills are very essential in the dating world. It isn't a question of whether or not you can get by without dancing skills, but how much better prepared you are to date with these skills.

5. *CHURCH.* Find a church to go to on Sundays that has a lot of young people in your age group. Sundays are usually the most unrushed of all the days of the week and will provide the atmosphere in which you can visit with one another and get to know each other. Get involved in a religious assignment that can bring you into association with others of your age.

6. *JOBS.* If you have options of several jobs, you may wish to pick a job where you will have greater opportunities to meet more people. For example, I know a girl that was an excellent secretary. She had the opportunity to work for a high official as a private secretary, but she turned it down and took a lower-paying job at an information window on a university campus to increase her chances of meeting fellows.

7. *BLIND DATES.* Everyone is of the opinion that everyone else hates blind dates. My questionnaires on the subject revealed that blind dates were not favored, but 76 percent of the fellows and 60 percent of the girls felt they were

O.K. once in a while. The biggest problem behind blind dating is its psychological stigma, because there seems to be the general feeling that a blind date is only used as a last resort, after all other efforts to get a date have failed.

The author has had the experience of creating several mixers to line people up. The popular fellows and the popular gals are usually most agreeable to work with you, and the ones that resent it the most are those that seldom date. It is part of their attitude and personality that makes them "undatables." They won't be lined up and they refuse to do anything that would encourage a fellow to ask them--and therefore they stay home.

To be more datable it helps immeasurably to be open to all kinds of suggestions. The datables are open to new ideas and new approaches. They are anxious to be introduced to people and even agree to be lined up.

Like everyone else, the author has had a few sad blind dates, but he has also had some that were outstanding and some that had the potential of becoming lasting relationships. The following hints may help to make blind dates more successful:

You will usually do better if the matchmaker has *your* best interest at heart and is not just trying to help out some other poor soul. Find out why the person thinks you would be such a great match. See a picture of the intended date if possible and get as much information as possible.

The typical approach is to double date with some friends and be introduced at the time of the date. This has some advantages, but the author would prefer to meet them directly or indirectly before committing himself to a date. When possible I have the matchmaker tell the person that I will be calling them. I call, and if I am at all impressed with the telephone conversation I attempt to meet them very informally that same evening or soon thereafter. Then and only then do I commit myself to a more formal date. I usually prefer not to double date with the common friends on the first date because they keep looking you both over to see how wonderfully you are getting along. I would rather meet them on my own terms.

The author has personally lined people up for blind dates who were later married as a result. It happens all the time, and so we should leave that avenue open for consideration.

8. *COMPUTERIZED DATING.* The world of automation seems to be trying to solve all of man's problems, even that of matchmaking. One study reported that there are over 1,000 computer-matchmaking services around the country. The author would like to think his other suggestions for finding dates are better than the machine approach, but if you have nothing else going and you can't see any dates forthcoming, it might be fun to try computerized dating occasionally. Many universities have an annual "computerized dance." It is yet another approach to meeting new people.

In summary:

Where can you go to get dates? The author has suggested that schools, universities and any kind of classes are excellent. It was also mentioned that active participation in a large variety of sports activities would be most helpful in meeting people. Go where people are, learn to mix with others and learn to move in new groups. If we were to sum up these suggestions into one small rule, it might go like this: **KEY 4: GO WHERE THE ACTION IS!**

PROBLEM 5: "HOW CAN A FELLOW INSURE GETTING A DATE EACH TIME HE TRIES?"

As you mix in groups and meet individuals that you feel you would like to date, make a list of them on paper. List their name, phone number and something about them. Most girls feel it is terrible that fellows keep lists, when they hear about it. It shatters the romantic idea of their position. But it is the only way a fellow can stay sane and successful in dating. Popular girls have their lists also, the only difference is that they have their long lists all written out on a calendar of scheduled dates.

The problem with waiting until you find just one girl that interests you and then asking her out, is that when you do work up the courage to ask her--she will likely be going steady with someone else, busy that week, or may have no interest in you. When you can't think of anyone else, it is most discouraging and depressing. It is always amazing how hard it is to think of a single prospect right after you failed with someone that you were extra excited about. However, if you have kept a list of potential dates, the list will quickly jar your memory and stimulate your recovery.

When you are just getting started in a new cycle of dating, it is not unusual at all to call five or more girls for one little date. This is no exaggeration. I have called many more than that on several occasions, and have observed many of my friends doing the same. Too often they give up after a few calls and become very dejected. They just can't think of anyone else to call. If they just had a little list of say ten girls or so with phone numbers, then it would give them the encouragement to remain determined until they have achieved a date whenever they want one. Many times I have said I wouldn't quit until I had a date, and the determination has paid off. And often that last girl on the list turns out to be first on the list the next time. The whole idea is so simple, but such an important key to successful dating--**KEY 5: KEEP A LIST OF POTENTIAL DATES!**

PROBLEM 6: "DON'T YOU NEED TO KNOW A PERSON FOR A GOOD WHILE BEFORE YOU DATE THEM?"

One of the worst things you can do with your intentions of dating someone is to put off doing it! We are naturally a little afraid to ask someone, especially when we are anxious about them. There will be times when we need to get to know them a little better to increase our chances of getting a date. But aside from this, the best time to act is now! If you are talking to a person you want to date and feel you have a positive response going with them, ask them right on the spot while the response is positive. Don't wait until you get home as so many do, when they don't have the eye contact and the positive forces working for them. Don't procrastinate.

The main reason we put it off is that we are scared, and not so mucn because we are really convinced that we will find a more suitable time. We need to challenge ourselves to have the guts that it takes. In my first years of dating, I saw a lot of girls that I wanted to date rather badly, but I was too afraid to ask them. Later I would see some of my friends get dates with them and it made me mad at myself for being less than they were. I made a *resolution* that *whenever I saw a girl that I was anxious to date, I would try.* And when I felt that frightened feeling coming I became even more determined and moved with greater speed to get the task accomplished. There were many times that I failed to come up with the date, but my successes were also increased and made it well worth the trouble. It also helped to build my courage and made me feel better about myself for going after the things in life that I wanted.

Some are never successful in dating because they will never venture to areas of chance and risk of failure. This applies to all areas of life! To sum this important rule up, you might say to yourself: "I challenge myself to have the guts to ask out every girl I feel some intensity of desire to date." This rule mainly applies to the fellows, but the same rule should also apply to the girls to give them a more outgoing personality and to encourage them to invite those fellows that they feel extra excited about to dinner or special events.

A person's success in dating will be greatly increased if they will put into effect **KEY 6: ACT NOW! DON'T PROCRASTINATE IN ASKING FOR DATES!**

HOW TO ASK FOR A DATE

(Section Mainly for Fellows)

ASKING IN PERSON VS. BY TELEPHONE: Most of the dating requests are via the telephone. Many prefer this method because the girl can't have as many ways of seeing how nervous they might be. They feel it gives them some protection behind the telephone. However, this works both ways. Girls feel like they can turn you down easier on the telephone. If you ask an individual in person, you will usually increase your chances of success. You can usually sell yourself better in person, if you have anything worth selling.

Another factor to consider here is that a very high percentage of people you ask might be individuals that you don't know very well. You may think that they know you simply because you are so impressed with them, but from experience I know it is most embarrassing when they *don't even recall your name!* They would be more likely to recognize you in person than over the phone, in cases like this. Fellows are often many steps ahead of the girl they are asking, and the girl may have given very little thought to the fellow and especially in considering them for a date. Appearing in person will give the girl a great deal more information as to who it is she is considering, so ask in person whenever possible.

WHAT WORDS TO USE IN ASKING FOR A DATE: Use the words that are natural to you! But for the purpose of aiding those who would appreciate a few possibilities we suggest the following:

It is best to first use a little "small talk" before breaking the sensational news that you want to date them. Ask them a few questions about anything. When possible ask them some significant questions about things that you might have in common. The masterful art of handling women is measured by your ability to get them to talk about themselves. Make a special effort to make them feel relaxed and that begins with being as relaxed as possible yourself. It is best to have a good conversation before asking them for a date, but the conversation should not go on for too long before getting to the point of asking them, especially if it is the first date. Some of the possible words you might use are:

1. "Hi Mary, this is Tom Miller calling. (Hi Tom) How are you doing? (O.K.) How are the studies coming? (Rather slow) Are you ready for the Chemistry test tomorrow? (I won't ever be ready for that.) How are you enjoying that class? (Well, it's not my favorite subject.) What do you think of the teacher? (He's too demanding.) Yea, I know what you mean. Well, say Mary, the reason why I called was that some of the fellows I go around with are planning a small cookout in the canyon this Saturday afternoon, and I was wondering if you would go with me? (That sounds fun Tom--I'd like to go!) Great! We were planning on leaving about 12:30 and being

gone most of the afternoon. How will that be? (That will be fine.) Good, we'll pick you up about 12:30, then, on Saturday. Don't study too hard! (Alright) Bye! (Bye!)"

2. After the small talk: "Well Mary, the reason I called was that I would like to take you to see a movie this Friday evening. (Oh, I'd like to Jim, but I've already made plans for that particular night.) Oh I see, well, would Saturday night be better for you? (It sure would.) Great! I'll pick you up about 8:00 P.M. We may be doubling with one of my friends, but I'm not sure yet."

3. The indirect and casual approach. You are just talking to a person about general things either on the phone or in person and then you tactfully lead the conversation around to some activity or event that you think you would like to take her to: "Do you ski, Mary? (I do some.) Do you enjoy skiing? How much skiing have you done? (I used to do a lot, but I don't seem to make it up on the slopes very much lately.) Say, we'll have to go up together sometime! (Watch for her response in word or facial expression.) (Yea, maybe we will.) Well, say I'm just looking for an excuse to go up this Saturday, how about it? (Sounds fun!) Good, I'll count on it then! I'll pick you up at 7:00 A.M. on Saturday."

The last approach is good when you can create the opportunity. It's purely casual and it just works itself into a date from a few questions, a few hints, or a little flirting and then the final commitment. Many girls will like the naturalness of the approach--it is not emotionally committing, but it is exciting and can often be a little romantic. Some may say "yes" before they realize they are accepting a date. It is great when you can get to the point that you become inventive and original and use different approaches every time. Then the job of getting dates becomes fun and less a chore. Remember that the words are not as important as being natural and relaxed.

HOW TO TURN A FELLOW DOWN
(Directed to the Girls)

Girls often worry a great deal about turning fellows down. Next to worrying about not getting asked, they probably worry most about the approach to use in turning someone away or telling them they're busy in a way that they will call back. To the fellows, it is hard to believe they are the least concerned when it seems that they cut us off so abruptly. The approach a girl should use depends on many things: your dating situation, how many times he has asked you and whether you would like him to call back in the future.

GOING STEADILY: If you are going very steadily with only one fellow, but there are no definite commitments, it would be helpful to tell the fellow who calls the truth: "Bill, I've been going a lot with just one fellow lately and haven't been accepting other dates." If you would like to date the person later, if nothing works out, you could say: "You can never tell what the future holds, if things don't work out, I hope you might consider calling back in the future." If you don't ever wish to date the fellow, leave off all encouraging lines!

If there is any one reason that sounds more justified to a fellow than other reasons, it would probably be that you are tied up with someone else and are not dating others.

YOU HAVE A DATE: If a fellow calls you up and you already have a date, but you are dying to go with the fellow, you'd better give him plenty of encouragement. There is a very high percentage of cases where fellows never call a second time. They may feel you don't want to go with them, or they may just get busy and never get around to it again. So if you want to go with them, say something specific to encourage it. One of the sharpest lines I have been given is: "That's the one night I am busy." This communicated to me that there were other nights that were available and I immediately proceeded to suggest another night.

If you are busy all seven nights of the week, don't let the poor fellow embarrass himself by going down all of the nights--you might say, after he has suggested two nights, something like: "Oh I'm sorry Henry, I've really got myself tied up the rest of this week."

"I'M BUSY" LINE: There are some expressions that fellows resent, and one of the most common is the line: "Oh, I'm busy." or "Sorry, I'm busy." That expression gets more use and means less than anything else you could possibly say. "Busy with who, what, why and how, you cat?" After so much dating a fellow soon learns that it is the universal line given for everything under the sun. He might later learn that the girl was genuinely tied up with another date but didn't really want to infer that she was dating someone else, but she was dying to go with him. Or, he finds out later that another girl who gave the same identical words wasn't busy at all, but would never accept a date with him. Fellows, as a result, exclaim that they wish that girls would be more direct and quit being so "cattie" and beating around the bush.

Most fellows would prefer some more information as to exactly what you mean when you say you are busy. If you have a date, why not say so; it might make the fellow feel that you are not just giving him the "brush off." You don't have to give all the details of why you are busy, but let him know that you have already committed yourself with some friends or another obligation. If you really want him to call back, encourage him by being "gracious" and "appreciative" of the call and "inviting" by telling him that you hope he calls again. But if you don't want him to call again, avoid all encouragement or excuses, and avoid thanking him for calling if you can. The author's sister had a roommate in college that used to actually ask the fellows to call again and lead them on and on with all kinds of encouraging lines. Then when she hung up she would say, "Oh I can't stand that creep, I wish he'd stop calling." Now isn't that bright? If you don't want to date him, remain vague and non-committing, and remain mostly quiet. When he says he'd better go, just say, "O.K., bye."

Many fellows will ask you directly if you're interested or if you should call back. I'd recommend even then that you remain vague, or you might say, "Well, I am very busy." I used to say, like other fellows, "I wish they'd be direct and come out and tell you they didn't want to date you." Finally I started asking them, and they told me, alright! I don't care how ruff and tuff a fellow pretends to be, it can be a real blow to his ego. He will remember you for a long, long time and every time he sees you he will remember how abrupt you were with him. And during his more depressed moments he will think of how totally he was rejected by an individual like you. It is still best to remain evasive and quiet with those that you don't want to date. The "busy line" is still the best for some calls.

GIRLS: ACCEPT ALL THE NEW DATES YOU CAN!

There are a few foolish girls who set up rigid guide lines that fellows must follow if they are going to accept a date with them. For example, they won't accept a date unless the fellow calls so many days in advance. They won't accept a date if they have any feeling they might be second choice. For special events they want two weeks of notification, etc. Assuming that you trust the fellow and would date him outside of your time schedule, you really ought to consider dating him and forgetting rigid time formats.

One girl I know gave me some very wise counsel once, that her mother had given her often: "Try to accept as many of the dates as you can, whether you are asked at the last minute or not--so long as you trust them. So what if you are the sixth girl he's called, maybe the next time you will be the first girl he calls. So what if you are not excited about him and have never thought of him as a date, he may surprise you and be much more fun than you thought."

I think this is excellent advice! Where does it get a girl to let pride stop her from becoming more popular and having more fun? Maybe the fellow you go with turns out to be a loser in your classification, but you may still come up a winner by meeting his friends. *You are always more attractive with someone than with no one.* "Wall flowers" just look less appealing than those who are dating many others. Once you get a dating cycle going and you are seen with many different fellows, it will give even more fellows the idea that you are datable. If you are never seen with anyone, your chances of being asked out are greatly lessened.

Remember that old fable that says, "Pride goes before the fall." Swallow your pride and have more success in dating. Be more pliable and accomodating and give every evidence you can that you are available. The author recalls time and time again that his most successful relationships developed from girls that he knew he could call on late and still experience success. Many times I would notify them the night before, the morning before, a few hours before, and even a few minutes before. I remember some exceptionally successful relationships where I felt welcome enough that I would just drop in on them without any notification occasionally and end up having a great time with them. I felt like I could drop in on the week nights or Saturday and Sunday afternoons; but I felt I had to call in advance if I wanted to drop in on Friday, Saturday and Sunday evenings, because of the likelihood of another fellow being there.

The author's experiences and the experiences of so many fellows he has talked to has verified that you never develop a meaningful relationship with a girl until you can break through the "ice" of formality and the formal date feeling. When you get to the point that you start thinking about them often and want to be in their company often, and feel welcome enough and comfortable enough to call them and tell them you are coming over in a few minutes, or just drop in on them, then you have a meaningful relationship that has the potential of going somewhere.

INTERESTING RESULTS OF QUESTIONNAIRES

In questions directed around the idea that girls should be more aggressive, the results were as follows: "Would you prefer that girls would be a little more aggressive in making their acquaintance?" The boys responded 62 percent *Yes,* 38 percent *No.*

The next question along the same line stated it this way: "If you were unsuccessful in getting a date, would you enjoy her calling you?" The boys responded with 84 percent *Yes,* 16 percent *No.* Even more surprising was that nearly half of the fellows questioned even approved of girls calling them that they hadn't made any advances toward: *Yes,* 45 percent; *No,* 55 percent. The thing that most fellows feared the most was having one girl continually calling them whom they weren't interested in.

The conclusion should still be that it is most suitable for the girls to leave most of the calling for the fellows, but give them encouragement and invite them to dinners when possible.

Another question was worded the following way: "Often a fellow wishes he had made a date, and although you do prefer more notice than a few hours, would you usually still be pleased to have him call?" Only 6 percent said *No;* 94 percent replied *Yes!* Other questions revealed that girls would prefer at least 2 days notice for a date and up to a week's notice when possible. What girls appeared to dislike the most was for a fellow to continually call them on the spare of the moment.

Over 92 percent of the fellows replied that they have been "hurt" by a girl at some time in their dating experience. In answer to another question, "Which do you fear the most: getting hurt or hurting the girl you are dating?" 42 percent listed that they feared hurting the girl the most and 58 percent feared getting hurt the most themselves. We often hold back from dating individuals because we are afraid of getting involved and getting hurt ourselves or hurting them; therefore we fear the risk and cut dating relationships short.

In conclusion, the author would suggest again the following keys to successful dating:

DEVELOP A DATING ATTITUDE!

1. *Stay in circulation!*
2. *Have less rigidity in our demands!*
3. *Develop a "play-tonic" attitude!*
4. *Go where the action is!*
5. *Keep a list of potential dates!*
6. *Act Now! Don't procrastinate in asking for dates!*

Chapter 2

WHERE TO GO ON A DATE

With 110 Fun Dating Activities

In the previous chapter we talked about the problems of how to get the date, and now we will talk about the first date, how to meet the person and how to make introductions. We will list some hints that will help the first date get started on the right foot. Then we will get into the main part of this chapter: the listing of over 100 fun dating activities. Too often dating becomes dull from lack of variety and imagination. The chapter will close with generalizations about the different types of dating activities listed and a comment on double dating.

GREETINGS AT THE FIRST DATE

You were successful in getting the date and now comes the moment of truth as you stand at the door to pick up the date. I don't care how many dates you have had or how long you have been dating, there is still a great moment of anticipation for both the boy and girl as you begin another first date. Sometimes it is just plain frightening and you wonder: "Will she be there?" "Is she as anxious as I am?" "What will she think of me?" "Could it be possible that this is the one that I've been waiting for?"

PUNCTUALITY: You can really get a date started wrong by being late. Both should be ready on time. Girls would be smart to be ready early and then keep themselves busy reading a book or playing a musical instrument, or something. It always takes longer to get ready than you anticipate, so it is best to start early. Fellows should make a special effort to be within five minutes of the appointed time. It is often difficult to anticipate the travel time, but if you are more than five minutes early, it would be best to take a drive until the time arrives. Individuals who are habitually late are not only very inconsiderate, they have a weakness in their character. However, if your date is late, don't let it spoil the evening--remain pleasant!

WHO GOES TO THE DOOR? It isn't all important who answers the door. Often it will be a member of the family or a roommate. But many fellows feel as I do, that it is always a little more special when you are greeted at the door by your date. You are a little uneasy at times anyway, and it is just a little more relaxing to meet that familiar face. And it makes you feel great to know that she considered you important enough to be ready on time.

PRECIOUSNESS OF A SMILE: First impressions are important, and if you can begin the first impression with the exchange of warm relaxed smiles, you have a lot going for you. The smile talks louder than anything you can say verbally with "Hello" or "Hi" or "How are you?"

I remember one date I had in college with a girl that I imagined great things for. I was taking her to a special dance and I had mentally visualized a warm greeting, but my visions were soon shattered. After being greeted by a roommate and waiting a short period of time, she finally came out of her room in a big hurry. She didn't look at me, say "hello" or even slacken her stride as she rushed towards the front door. The evening was started with just a slight letdown.

Then I remember the poise of some other girls who came out and greeted me genuinely and warmly with a smile. That precious moment when eyes meet and linger for a short time gives you a real boost, and you get the feeling that you are accepted and that things are going to be great. It also relaxes you and is often the moment that begins a romance.

INTRODUCTIONS

To keep the atmosphere relaxed, girls, don't go rushing out the front door too abruptly. If it is convenient with parents or roommates, take a minute to introduce your date to them. Everyone seems to forget how to introduce someone else, especially at the moment that it needs to be done. The easiest way to remember the proper method of introduction is to *always mention the name of the person that you wish to honor the most!*

THREE HELPFUL RULES:

a. Mention an important person first: "President Smith, I would like you to meet my mother."
b. Mention an older person first: "Mother, I would like you to meet my friend Jack."
c. Mention a lady before a man: "Mrs. Jones, I would like you to meet Mr. Brown."

Sometimes it doesn't seem natural to repeat the second half of the introduction. Sometimes you reverse the order just to get the other persons' attention who might be in another group. Sometimes it is hard to decide whose name to put first. Don't stand there trying to figure out all the formalities, just start introducing any way it comes out. The important thing is to do it in a relaxed manner and help others to become friends. After you have mentioned the names it is often appropriate to mention something that will help identify the two individuals to each other. Mention something they both have in common, or say anything that will relax the two individuals.

VISITING WITH PARENTS OR ROOMMATES: If the girl is living at home with her parents, it is quite common for the father to want to visit with her date for a moment while she completes her last-minute touches in getting ready. Many fellows dread the thoughts of getting "worked over" by the dad, but really, this should be an expected part of the dating cycle. A positive relationship with parents is so essential to everyone's happiness. Parents have invested a lot of time, money and hopes in the happiness of their daughter and they have every right in the world to become somewhat acquainted with the creature that is taking her out.

Speaking as a fellow I have always enjoyed staying at the home a few minutes. I learn a lot about the girl by seeing her in her own environment and how she responds to her parents. I like to see her mother and get a general idea of what she will look like in 30 years. Occasionally, on a first date where I don't really know the girl very well, I have purposely set the time of the date to provide a few minutes to visit.

Some fellows are very uncomfortable in front of others and would prefer to leave quickly. Some girls also feel awkward staying and want to get away from the mad house of screaming kids or parental pressure. While keeping these personal preferences and various situations in mind first, consider staying just a little longer in the home.

IMPORTANCE OF A COMPLIMENT: Sometime during your greetings, or visit, or early in the date you should have found something that is deserving of a compliment. I don't know how many times I have spent the whole afternoon washing and waxing the car, and I have waited for the girls I dated to say something, but they hardly ever do until I tell them. Likewise the fellow should be more observant of the girl's appearance. She has probably spent a lot of time with her hair, or paid good money to get an operation performed on it; or, she has just made or bought a new dress--and how many fellows ever notice any of these things? They may both end up spending the evening in silence, wondering why the other is so unobservant.

The whole idea of dating is to create some meaningful friendships, so *use every opportunity possible to be observant, sensitive, perceptive, and appreciative of what the other person does or may have done!*

PLAN & DECIDE AHEAD

We could be more successful in dating if we would plan for success. Some never know what they are going to do before a date, and are not sure what they have done when they're through. Some have the philosophy that it is better to "ad-lib" and do what seems best at the moment. It is great to be as relaxed and flexible as possible, but a tentative plan can give a real meaningful structure for a successful date, and yet it can still be altered as needed.

Plan ahead to go to interesting places, do interesting things and have an interesting conversation. If you haven't dated a lot, it would help to write down a list of things to do and talk about. Then when the time comes you will be more natural and spontaneous. *Attempt to be original and creative in the things you do.* But no matter what the date is, even if it is just going to a movie, you would be smart to get the paper out and decide ahead of time the movies you would like to see. Plan ahead, because it is more difficult to think of things and make decisions when you are under pressure in front of someone that you are trying to impress.

Girls like fellows who are leaders and who can make decisions. Many girls have a real aversion to making the decisions. So fellows, even if you are very anxious to take them where they would like to go, stop forcing the decision upon them! You be ready to decide!

On the other hand, girls should remember that some fellows are not good decision makers. And other fellows may be overly zealous to please them to the point that they insist that the girl choose the movie or activity. So girls, make your tentative decisions also as to which movie or activity you would enjoy. Remember however, that the fellow may ask you only out of courtesy. Most will feel the obvious pressure to at least ask, so it is best to hold back a little until he becomes more insistent. Give him plenty of room to make the decision before taking over the decision making.

Example: "What show would you like to see Mary?" "Oh, I don't care, which one would you like to see?" "I want you to pick one, Mary." "Well, two movies I thought might be fun were...." "Which one looks best, Mary?" "Well, I guess I would most prefer...."

A very common complaint of fellows is that girls won't help in choosing dating activities. If your fellow insists that you make some of these decisions, be ready to offer some alternative suggestions first, and final decisions only at his continued insistence.

A word to the guys:

If you are trying to impress a girl, don't take her out for a big time in places and situations where you aren't comfortable. Get her into the arena that you are familiar with, turn the conversation to the areas in which you have some knowledge. Do the things that you feel natural about, and your chances of impressing her will be greatly increased.

DIVERSITY IN DATING

One of the greatest challenges a fellow has in the dating world is to come up with new and different activities. It becomes so boring to both the fellow and girl to have the same old dates every time. It isn't so bad on the first date, but after you have had a few dates with the same person it becomes difficult to think of new things. I don't know how many times I have seen fellows sitting around trying to come up with something new and different.

If daters will utilize the list of activities which follows with some real concentration, this list alone will make this book very valuable and worthwhile in creating real successful dating! It isn't that the list itself is so special, but it should help to stimulate your imagination and serve as a challenge to really do new things that you have never done before. It will not only expand your own horizons, but your dating life will become very refreshing. It won't be hard to add to this list. All you have to do is walk into a sporting goods store, or read the newspaper about something that is about to take place in your community. Become involved in new and exciting activities and you will enrich your life.

This list will become more meaningful if you will mark those activities that you think you would like to use. Use any code that will be helpful to you, but the following is a suggestion to consider:

Rate 1 to 3:

1. Will do in the immediate future.
2. Will attempt to make arrangements and work into dating life sometime.
3. May consider, but not overly anxious about.
   (Those that you are not interested in you could leave blank.)

110 FUN DATING ACTIVITIES

I. SPORTING DATES:

1. Tennis
2. Badminton
3. Volleyball
4. Horseshoes
5. Swimming
6. Water skiing
7. Snow skiing
8. Table Tennis
9. Bowling
10. Roller-skating
11. Ice skating
12. Golf
13. Miniature golf
14. Hiking
15. Mountain climbing
16. Fishing
17. Flying kites
18. Pool
19. Shuffle board
20. Croquet
21. Darts
22. Boating
23. Canoeing
24. Sailing
25. Shooting guns
26. Archery
27. Hunting birds & Animals
28. Camping out
29. Cook-outs
30. River runs--rapids
31. Tubing on rivers or snow
32. Surfing
33. Flying
34. Karate lessons
35. Judo lessons
36. Baseball
37. Jogging
38. Motorcycling
39. Bicycling
40. Tobogganing

Spectator Sports:

41. Baseball
42. Basketball
43. Hockey
44. Football
45. Car races
46. Horse races
47. Boat races
48. Boxing matches
49. Wrestling matches
50. Golf tournaments, etc.

II. SOCIAL DATES:

51. Parties of all sorts!
52. Visit family & relatives
53. Visit friends
54. Parlor games
55. Thought games
56. Box games--"Monopoly," etc.
57. Cooking--taffy, pop corn, etc.
58. Home movies, slides, photos
59. Play records and recordings
60. Sing-alongs by Piano, etc.
61. School socials
62. Club, Fraternities & Sororities
63. Participation in civic project
64. Political campaigning
65. Go out to dinner--commercial
66. Invite others to dinner
67. Go dancing--ballroom
68. Square and folk dancing
69. Go to a movie; watch T.V.
70. Double & Group dates!

III. CULTURAL & INTELLECTUAL DATES:

71. Plays or dramatic productions
72. Musicals
73. Opera & Ballet
74. Join a Choir or musical group
75. Play instruments
76. Learn a duet
77. Recitals & concerts
78. Art gallery
79. Museums
80. Paint or Paint-by-number
81. Make a mosaic, etc.
82. Work on a puzzle
83. Sightseeing tours
84. Zoo
85. Industrial plants--factories
86. Wildlife preserves, fish hatcheries
87. State capitol
88. Planetarium
89. Visit famous historical places
90. Study date for school
91. Take a class together
92. Courtship class
93. Read a book together
94. Lyceums & forum assemblies
95. Profession speakers
96. Debates
97. Pick a topic & study it.
98. Invent something
99. Write something
100. Crossword puzzles

IV. RELIGIOUS:

101. Go to church services
102. Youth fireside chats
103. Youth gatherings
104. Religious classes
105. Read scriptures together
106. Read religious book
107. Church socials
108. Church service projects
109. Organize religious study group
110. Visit sick, help someone

IDEAS FOR OTHER DATES

It should be helpful now to discuss some aspects of the preceding list of dating activities. As was mentioned, the list is not all inclusive. With just a little awareness of happenings in your own area, you could be much more specific and come up with many sporting events, social and musical events that the author has not listed.

I. SPORTING DATES:

At least 50 different types of sporting activities have been listed that would make excellent dates and certainly there are many more. Every geographic area has sporting events that are distinctive to that area.

If you are one of the few who claim not to like sports at all, then you have cut your potential dating activities in half. Sure you can get by without them, but you will greatly increase your dating potential if you can develop an interest in at least a few sporting activities. Girls are usually the ones who feel awkward and therefore shun sports. The thing to do is to gain a little self-confidence in the world of sports, and this comes simply by being involved in sporting activities. The more time you spend, the better you will become. You will also soon learn that you really don't have to be very good at anything--it is more a matter of enjoying yourself and accepting your abilities as they might be. Sports become extremely competitive among boys, but when they are a dating activity, they are usually entered into more with the spirit of game and sheer fun. Although a fellow may prefer a little competition, he doesn't really expect a girl to beat him. In fact, some boys are so egotistical about their athletic prowess that a girl would be wise not to beat them, or at least not very often!

There are always sporting activities that you can participate in vicariously--by watching. Successful daters usually include all of their school's main sports, like football and basketball. This can start with high school and continue on through college and even the professional teams. This, of course, is the least strenuous method of involvement in sports.

For the more "ambitious," there are usually places that you can play table tennis, bowl, and play miniature golf. These are usually simple enough for everyone to enjoy. And most individuals can invest enough to buy a tennis racket and ball to play real tennis. If you find it hard to do many of these you can at least buy a dart board and throw darts.

Any experience that requires roughing it and "letting your hair down" can be one of the greatest dating experiences you will ever have. It reveals a lot about a person's personality that lays hidden in the more formal and structured situations. When people become physically exhausted, when they are under stress or strain, you can see how they stand up under pressures and learn how pleasant they really are. You discover how selfish they are with their own needs and comforts. Any couple that is serious with each other ought to plan some strenuous activities from time to time.

From questionnaires we found that the kind of dating activities both fellows and girls seem to rate the highest as their "most fun" dates are in the "out-of-doors": a canyon party, a cookout and water sports. There is always something special about getting out with the beauties of nature that people remember and it seems to add to the romance of dating.

II. SOCIAL DATES:

Under "social dates" we listed all parties together as just one item and various games as three items, but there is literally no end to the kinds of parties you can plan with friends and take turns in sponsoring at your home, and there are literally hundreds of games that you can play. Most bookstores carry several books on games you can play in groups. And you can buy a lot of fun in some boxes, as new games are always being invented. The old "stand-bys" are always worth their time, such as checkers, chess and Monopoly. If you don't have a book or any box games, it doesn't take much creativity to make up some games.

Get a piece of string and blow up a balloon and bat it back and forth like volleyball. Get a cup of flour with a penny in the bottom, tip it upside-down on a plate. Then take a knife and take turns cutting away the flour. The one to cut it when the penny falls, loses. Some make them pick up the penny with their teeth! Throw or roll pennies against the wall to see who can get the closest. These are just examples of things you can create with practically nothing.

It can be a real fun evening just visiting with the family of either partner, or visiting friends or relatives. It is always fun as dates to get in the kitchen and make something together. It may be candy, pop corn, tacos, a pie or practically anything.

There are always dances being held somewhere, for special occasions or on a weekly basis. Make an attempt to go to the school dances, they will always be a special date to remember. Then again, there is always a movie.

SHOWS: Of all the dating activities, shows or movies are by far the most common. The questionnaires indicated that over 65 percent of all early dating was going to shows. There is nothing wrong with going to a show--it is one of the better dating activities. You cannot always be sure that your date will go for a new idea, but you can usually count on the fact that she has been taken to a lot of shows and will probably enjoy another one. If you feel uncertain of yourself and don't know what to talk about, shows can be a great protection for a shy person. If you don't enjoy your date, maybe you can at least enjoy the movie!

The disadvantages of shows are that you should be dating a person to get to know him or her, and if you go to a show you will be limiting that opportunity a great deal. How many times have you had a date like the following: You pick up the girl and rush off to the show, you get out of the show and go straight home. If you are on a first date, it seems rather awkward to stay in the car and talk much, so you take your date to the door and that's it. Big date?

Action after the show: So often a fellow waits until after the show to suggest some other activity, but many girls are too rigid to allow a fellow to add more to the date and will often give an excuse that they need to get home. This can always be a big letdown for a fellow. To increase the chances of doing something after the show, you should tell them as you pick them up that you were planning something afterwards. Even a better time to tell them is when you initially ask them for the date. After they have accepted the idea of a movie, you can simply add that afterwards you will be going over to a friends for ice cream, etc. If you aren't sure of the activity, simply state that you will probably do something small after the show. Then they will anticipate it and it won't become awkward later on.

A good movie can make a great date, but if a girl has had three show dates in the same week it can really be a drag, especially if she has started repeating movies. Going to shows all the time suggests that you have no imagination. Try to be more creative than being a "showboy" all the time!

III. CULTURAL & INTELLECTUAL DATES:

If you are near a university there are always lots of outstanding plays, musicals and special programs that make just *outstanding* dates for a small cost. If you have an activity card they may cost you nothing. It would be hard to find more worthwhile dating activities than some of these performances. In addition to university performances, there are always the professional groups that come to every community.

Every geographical area has some famous historical places that seem to be visited only by tourists. My father was raised within a few miles of the Great Salt Lake in Utah but never swam there until later in life. There must be a famous cave, a famous historical place that could make an interesting date. Visit a park or zoo, the planetarium or a museum. Paint a small picture together, "by-the-numbers" if need be. Write something together or try to invent something. Or, if you both need to study for classes, go somewhere and have a study date.

One of the best ways to get to know someone is to get on a work project together. It might be a service project, a research paper or thesis, or something you are making or building. If you can do something together that will give you a sense of accomplishment, the dates will be more fulfilling. Too often we think that dates have to be all fun and games. This is a phony atmosphere, because in married life you do more work together than play, and what you need to know about a person is how well you can work together and solve problems. So when it is possible, try to find some project you can work on together. However, be careful that the project doesn't go on forever and consume all of your spare time together or it may put undue stress on your relationship.

IV. RELIGIOUS DATES:

If you want a relationship where there is faith and trust, if you would like to keep it on a high moral plane, if you want a partner that believes in God, then you need to spend some of your dating time in a religious realm. Everyone ought to be in church anyway, so why not kill two birds with one stone and take a date with you? It will add a new dimension to your relationship as you begin to think in spiritual terms towards each other. Some people can never get their minds off the more physical aspects of the opposite sex. If you take them to church you are more apt to respect them and to see another side to the person. Sunday is a beautiful time to be dating, especially when it is going to church. It gives you something different to build your relationship on.

Some of the most rewarding dates that I have had have been times when I have sat down and read the scriptures or some good church book with a young lady. I have always preferred to take turns reading the pages aloud, but some prefer to read them silently and then make comments on them. You can't do this with everyone, but as your relationship deepens, you will probably feel the need to add this kind of spiritual dimension.

Even though there aren't many religious activities listed, it has been in this area that the author has spent a large percentage of his dates. If you belong to a real active church group that has a good youth program, there is no end to the amount of time you can spend in church meetings, church socials, outings and promotions. Just make sure that your date is as enthusiastic about church functions as you are!

DOUBLE DATING

There are pros and cons to double dating, as in most things. We will mention some of the negative aspects first. Some girls are just big flirts, and it seems more natural to them to flirt with your buddy than with you. Some girls talk too much to the other girls to the exclusion of their dates. I remember one double date where the girls carried on special coded finger language between themselves all evening. I soon learned that there were some girls that I had to date alone in order to get my share of the attention! The disadvantages to the fellow can also reverse themselves for the girls.

I had one set of friends that got so friendly with their partner's date that they both agreed to change partners right in the middle of the date! Double dating can also be more difficult to arrange. It is always easier to get two people together than it is four or six people.

Some of the advantages of double dating are that you get to see your date in a different light. Some are entirely different on a double date than they are with you alone. You see how they respond to others and you quickly learn from others what they think of your date.

One of the biggest reasons for doubling is that it expands your horizons. In doubling you seek broader levels of activities and a larger variety at the same time. You get to know more people and may meet others that you could become interested in. Another advantage to doubling is that you can learn from others by watching them react successfully in a dating situation. It becomes important that you seek out high quality friends, whose characteristics are worthy of emulation.

When you tell a friend that you would like to double with them, you are paying them a great compliment. And there is a law of multiple persons which says, in essence, that two people working together can do more than twice what either of them could do alone. What this means is that they spur each other on in a positive way, they provide in each other a stimulus that makes them more powerful, more dynamic and more successful. The author's experiences with these great groups have proved these principles to be true many times.

One group in particular stands out in my mind above the rest, and this was a group in high school. When they invited me into their group it was one of the greatest experiences of my life. We were always coming up with things to do in the group. Our particular church didn't have a newspaper, so we volunteered to put it out and would meet weekly to accomplish this little service project. We did a lot of double dating together and it was always our goal to come up with something different. One time we told our dates that we were taking them out to dinner, but naturally we didn't say where. It just happened that we had to stop at the home of one of the fellows. When we got them all in, we took our dates out into the kitchen where there were bags of groceries and told them we were hungry. We then went into the other room to enjoy each other's company while they cooked. It really turned out to be a lot of fun for everyone, believe it or not!

Another time we did nearly the same thing, only this time the fellows fixed the most inviting meal you could imagine. It had some most unusual and tasty arrangements, all fixed by a group of high school boys! Then there were the Sunday study group dates where we would get together and show slides or take turns leading the discussion about some religious topic. Everything was wholesome, clean and beautiful. Mixing in these kinds of groups made it easy to keep ourselves clean. Life wasn't a "dirty joke"--it was something beautiful, fun and worthwhile. What a contrast the author found when he soon left for the army! There he met very few men who had anything wholesome or worthwhile to say about womanhood.

The author is convinced that it is worth the extra effort to double date and to mix in groups that elevate you and give you a true perspective for a dating life that you can always cherish with fond memories.

The very common problem, then, that the author has attempted to deal with, is that of *how to make each new date exciting and enjoyable.* So many fellows and gals are concerned about making a good first impression. The author hopes the suggestions offered are of some help. But remember to just be yourself, and if you would be successful in your dating, apply **KEY 7: ADD VARIETY TO YOUR DATING!**

Chapter 3

DEEPENING THE RELATIONSHIP

We have covered the areas of getting a date and where to go on dates, but there is much more to building a relationship than simply going places. The process of developing and deepening the relationship is a very involved one and covers so much material that we have divided the chapter into three main sections: *Section I* deals with the initial development of the relationship, *Section II* covers the more physical aspects of romance, and *Section III* handles getting involved with your companion in his or her daily life, and progresses to the point of small commitments.

SECTION I

DEVELOPMENT OF THE RELATIONSHIP

EXPECTATION & EMOTIONAL LEVELS ON EARLY DATES

Successful dating can be greatly increased by understanding the expectation and emotional levels of those you are dating. Fellows are prone to be more anxious than the girls because of the fact that they are usually the initiators of the date. Many times a fellow has been thinking about dating a girl over a long period of time and may have developed a real "crush" on a girl. He often begins to plan ahead for what they will do on future dates and how he will try to win her heart. If he is really excited about the person, his imagination runs wild with anticipation of engagement and marriage. Sound crazy? It is crazy, but it really happens when a fellow is strongly infatuated.

And what is the girl thinking all this time? She may be trying to figure out why she even accepted the date. She may hardly know the fellow and certainly had never thought of ever dating him. She may have been caught off guard and accepted the date partly because she didn't quite know how to say "no." Or maybe she didn't have anything better to do. In any event, her thoughts may present an awkward contrast to the excited thoughts of the fellow. The situation could be reversed, but the tendency is for the fellow to be far ahead of the girl in his emotional involvement. To put it in the vernacular of baseball, the fellow might be on second or third base while the girl hasn't reached first base in the ball park of emotional involvement.

Understanding these facts can help a relationship a great deal. Many times you hear girls say that they think fellows are awfully forward and try to move too fast. It would help if the girl could understand the potential feelings a fellow might have for them. You see, a fellow will usually ask a girl for a date because he is strongly attracted to her. As one fellow put it, in a discussion group on dating: "I ask a girl for a date when she turns me on enough that I feel I could enjoy kissing her." So if you wonder why fellows appear too forward, it is because they are often at a high emotional level, whereas the girl may not be.

It would help a relationship if a fellow would realize the more likely position of the girls and stop trying to rush them so much in the areas of romancing at first. Fellows should not become discouraged so quickly when they find that the girls are not as excited about them as they are towards the girls. It usually takes a girl a date or two to develop an interest in a fellow that she hadn't personally been interested in before the first date. So in conclusion, it will be helpful to understand the various expectation and emotional levels of those that we are dating.

PROBLEM 8: "HOW MANY SHOULD I DATE AT A TIME?"

There are many different philosophies on how to approach dating. Some date one person until they are totally dissatisfied with them and then they concentrate on just one other person. Others approach it by dating two or three at a time. Still others take the shotgun approach and date about as many as they can possibly crowd in. The author has tried all of them and has observed that some approaches work better than others. However, it seems that young daters, and those without any special feelings for any particular person, would be wise to play the field and gain experiences with as many as possible. Then as you get to the age and time where you want to get serious, you should obviously narrow down the field. If no one person stands out, then try to eliminate it down to two or three individuals that seem to be the most outstanding. Date them and compare your feelings about them in an effort to narrow the field down to one person.

A paradox in the dating world is that very young daters often become serious with the first ones they date and narrow their field far too rapidly, when they should be gaining experience with many. Then the "old timers" that are still single tend to play the field too broadly and are all too slow in narrowing the field and developing a deeper and meaningful relationship.

The idea of trying to narrow your field can obviously be more easily accomplished by the fellows than it can by the girls, but the girls can also control their approach, by saving dates for those that mean the most to them.

MERRY-GO-ROUND: There are a few that seem to get overly involved and serious with everyone that comes along, but most of us find ourselves going endlessly from one to another, always hoping to find something better. If you are on this merry-go-round, try and get off for a while and center in on a few special individuals and eventually one. Pick someone and try to develop a meaningful relationship with them. Some of us have difficulty in getting married simply because we don't know how to develop a deep and meaningful relationship with someone. Our friendships are too flighty, too brief and too much on the surface to ever take on the kind of meaning that produces a marriage.

To summarize, a successful dater usually knows how to play the field, but he knows when to start narrowing the field and how to develop deeper and more meaningful friendships.

KEY 8: NARROW THE FIELD IN PYRAMID FASHION!

Here is a list of questions that you might consider asking yourself that may help in deciding if you are going with a person that you really could marry:

1. Do you feel the emotions of love and affection for them?
2. Are you proud to be seen with them?
3. Do they have religious views and goals that compare with your own?
4. Do you trust their word and their ability to remain faithful to you?
5. Do you have a lot in common intellectually and educationally?
6. Are you anxious to be with them and do you miss them when you aren't with them for many days?
7. Girls: Do you have confidence that he could provide well for you and be a good father?
   Boys: Do you have confidence in their being a good housemaker and mother of your children?
8. Do you feel jealousy at the thoughts of someone else being with them or taking over?
9. Do you have a lot in common, do you share similar views and have the same values?
10. Are you usually happy together or do you spend most of your time arguing?
11. Does the person challenge you or give you a motivation to be a better person?
12. Do you like to do things for the person?
13. Are you comfortable and impressed with their parents?

14. Does the person help and encourage you in your life's goals?
15. Does the person have an even and cherry disposition?
16. Does the person have confidence in themselves and faith in their own destiny?
17. Is the person considerate of your needs and feelings?
18. Is he a gentleman to you and others; or is she lady-like?
19. Do you have comparable economic needs that can be satisfied?

PROBLEM 9: "HOW CAN I TELL IF I'M STUCK ON ONE PERSON TOO LONG?"

One of the biggest challenges in dating is making a decision on how you feel about those that you date. If you haven't dated the person very long, then the obvious is that you should continue to date them a little longer and gather more information upon which to make the decision. But assuming that you are old enough to get serious about marriage and you still find yourself perplexed about making the decision, what then?

It is relatively easy to determine that some are "deadwood," but what about the rest that you have fond feelings for, want to be with them, but don't feel certain enough to commit yourself to marriage? You may know that they are great individuals and everyone tells you they are good for you. You may also wish to be married in the worst way, but you still wonder if they are the right one.

I have personally dated individuals for long months and even years with whom I was ready to move into the committing stages of courtship, but they, on the other hand, were not sure in their minds if I was the right one for them! I have also been on the other side of that agonizing fence, where I deeply appreciated the person and felt a great deal of love for them and spent many emotional hours attempting to make a decision to marry them. However, I was unable to feel at peace inside in making a marriage decision. And yet I still thought so much of them that I really didn't want to stop our relationship. So, on and on it went for long periods of time, with both of us living with a hope that time would be the cure and that I (or they) could eventually feel right about it. To those not in our situation or especially those already married or even those going steady, our situation was ridiculous and foolish! We ought to just simply make up our minds and move ahead with marriage plans! Some well-meaning friends were even obnoxious enough to attempt to push us. It is more easily said than done, to individuals who are trying to be entirely honest with themselves and their emotions. You just can't move ahead when your feelings and emotions are so uncertain. You don't feel good dropping them and you don't feel good "yet" about getting married.

One cannot go on living in "indecision" forever. We all have a breaking point, a time when we cannot endure indecision any longer. The author experienced such a time after pursuing one person for years, when he finally felt that for reasons of sanity, he had to declare to her that her indecision was his decision that it was not right. I knew personally that I would not have been happy marrying someone that had proceeded in uncertainty. I determined that my own ego and entire self-image could not survive or find joy with someone who was not sure they wanted me.

One thing that may help in making a decision is to try to progress into some stage of commitment with each other and then continue to work on further commitments, in something similar to the following order:

1. Be with each other a great deal of every week.
2. Save certain special dates for each other.
3. Reserve at least one night or more a week as the night for the two of you.
4. Be with each other nearly every day for a period of time; do as much as you can possibly do in studying, working and eating together.
5. Officially go steady and turn down all other dates.
6. Accept a pin to certify that you are going steady.
7. Accept a friendship ring to signify some degree of commitment to each other.
8. Become engaged to be married, but keep it between you for 1 to 4 weeks.

9. Accept an engagement ring and announce your engagement soon after.
10. Get married.

If you find you cannot continue to progress, show a little patience, but after so many months of no progress, you need to break it off! **KEY 9: MAKE A DECISION WITH THOSE YOU HAVE INDECISION!**

BREAKING UP & PERSONAL EMOTIONS

PROBLEM 10: "WHEN DO I BREAK UP A RELATIONSHIP?"

Assuming now that you have made tentative decisions about your boy or girl friends, and you find that several are "hopeless cases" for further dating, then your next step is to decide when and how to break it off with them. This is not always easy, since feelings are involved. There are many times when it just seems good to have someone to date that you enjoy being with, whether you feel you could marry them or not. There may be situations which may justify this approach for brief periods; however, if you are of marriageable age, the real goal of dating is to find someone that means everything to you and one with whom you can deepen a relationship to the point of marriage, eventually. If you are dating someone that you know you won't consider for marriage, then you are not having real success in your dating! You are not really being honest with yourself or them. In fact, there is probably no worse kind of dishonesty that you can indulge in than to lead someone on with false hopes and to wrongfully involve their emotions and love over long periods of time.

Some feel that if you confess to your date your questionable belief in any future, you are then justified in dating them. Leveling with them will lessen the dishonesty, but a good measure of the evil is still present, because a heart in love can never give up hope that things will change! They still operate with false hopes and vain dreams. You are still robbing them of time and the sacred emotions of hope and love. You are never doing them a favor by continuing to date them. *The sooner you can break up, the better it will be for both of you.* It is not easy, your feelings of dependance may tear you apart, but you must break! You can usually remain friends, and by all means assure them of your concern for them as individuals.

But in conclusion, another basic key to successful dating is **KEY 10: CUT OFF "DEADWOOD" AS SOON AS POSSIBLE!**

PROBLEM 11: "HOW DO I BREAK OFF A RELATIONSHIP?"

We are sometimes so deeply involved in our search for our dream person that we trample on those that don't measure up to our demands. We can do it without really knowing that we are doing it. They may even be individuals that we have never dated or dated very little, or maybe we have dated them for a while but never realized that they were seriously involved.

I have known many fellows and a few girls who never date unless they are exceptionally interested in the person. They may not date for many months until they finally find someone that strongly appeals to them. Obviously this kind of person may have a lot at stake emotionally if they are turned down. I have known some that have taken it very bitterly and have allowed it to depress them for weeks at a time. Can you imagine what goes on in their minds, the feelings of dejection and lack of worth, the feeling of the futility in life? They were counting too strongly on that brief moment of success and some kind of acceptance, and had built themselves up to an emotional peak.

I am convinced that there isn't anything in the world more emotionally involving than dating. If you are selling and lose a sale, you can always blame the product; but when you are offering yourself to someone else and they reject you, it can be quite earth-shaking!

Someone can have a real bad crush on you whom you have never really dated before. They might have been dreaming about you for months on end, with the exaggerated ideas that only a love-struck individual can concoct. And through all of this you could be completely unaware and oblivious to their emotional trauma. As they present themselves to you for dating, they are awkward and unimpressive and you naturally determine not to accept them. But what are you supposed to do? You may do the right thing in rejecting them, but be so very careful *how* you do it!! When it seems at all appropriate, leave the door open for the future. When it seems prudent to close the door on future opportunities of dating that person, close it, but *close it all so gently and with kindness and respect for the individual.* Remember that the individual is a child of God and is therefore as worthy of receiving kindness and respect as you are. Allow them to retain their own self-esteem. *Let them know that you are honored by their interest in you,* but that you are tied up with others at the time.

Why should the author belabor this area so? Maybe it is because he himself has been torn assunder a few times during those agonizing moments of defeat when the cutting crudeness of some has sapped every seeming reason for living. "Oh, for just a moment of consideration; if only for a second, a voice of acceptance of my being!"

Maybe the author talks about it because there have been a few moments in his life when he has found himself acting as the ruthless destroyer of proffered esteem. He too has found himself perplexed at how to handle such delicate moments.

Maybe the author is concerned because he has had brief acquaintance in two situations with fellows who became so deeply and emotionally involved that they lost all rationale and actually murdered those who had rejected them, and one took his own life immediately afterwards. The other fellow had never dated the girl, but wanted to very badly. These situations are not totally alone in the world. You read of them every year in the newspapers, where some boyfriend kills his girlfriend, or a husband kills his wife and then takes his own life. A large number of murders are a direct result of broken hearts and disappointed love. So many people in mental institutions were driven there from emotional situations that involved the simple little word "love."

Why mention such cases? Only to emphasize how deeply involved some individuals are with their loves. And if many commit murder, how many others are near that destroying point? How many others are suffering emotional scars that will remain with them throughout their lives? And how many remaining ones are stripped of their personal pride and self-image?

If you would like to be unfavorably remembered for a long time, just be crude and inconsiderate to someone that has some emotional appreciation for you. You can be rather excited about a person temporarily, and their rudeness will cause you to forget them immediately, and you could care less about them from then on. But if your interest in them runs very deep and if it has gone on for very long; if your emotional expectations have been strongly committed to them, then rudeness can become a very personal thing. It is as if they are attacking you personally and it is more difficult to convince yourself that they are all that you had dreamed them to be.

I have dated hundreds of girls and I don't even remember many of their names or much of anything about them. I do remember relatively well, however, certain girls that rejected me too abruptly. Some of them I never even got to first base with, and some cut me off abruptly before I was ready. Then there were those that I dated for long periods of time about whom I will always carry mixed feelings of appreciation and despair for the rejection I felt with them. It has never ceased to amaze me how one can care for a person so greatly over periods of time, but if they are the ones that lead out in the severing of the relationship, you can never quite forgive them--even if you are later convinced that it was a great blessing. I have seen the same thing with girls I have taken the lead in breaking up with. I continue to appreciate them and want so badly to be their friends, but I am made strongly aware that they never do appreciate me quite the same as I do them. If there are emotional overtones, it is better to just leave them alone than try to build a Platonic friendship. This kind of friendship becomes offensive and repulsive to them because of their previous anticipation of so much more. So much for the paradoxes of life.

In summary, then, remember that emotions do run very deep. And you can never tell who it is that might be emotionally involved with you. Remember also that: *LENGTH OF TIME HAS LITTLE TO DO WITH THE INTENSIFICATION OF EMOTION BY A VIVID IMAGINATION!!* Remember too that some feel things more deeply than others. Treat everyone with respect and kindness whether they are seeking their first date, their 100th date or their last. This includes the boys asking the girls or the girls trying to get the attention of the fellows in their own way. Leave the door open for the future when possible, but when it seems prudent that you should close the door permanently, do so, but be sure to apply **KEY 11: CLOSE DOORS GENTLY! HANDLE WITH CARE THOSE WHO ARE EMOTIONALLY INVOLVED!**

PROBLEM 12: "CAN A PERSON GET TOO INVOLVED IN KINDNESS?"

Another of the paradoxes of dating is that at times we are not kind and considerate when we should be, but we are overly kind at other times, to our own detriment. So many dates are never made, out of fear of hurting someone, and too many relationships are cut short from fear of getting involved and causing emotional pain.

In this book I have belabored the importance of kindness and consideration, because it is so lacking at important moments. However, when it comes to finding a date, don't allow your fears of hurting someone to stop you altogether! The writer is convinced that we could become infinitely more successful in dating if *we would date those we have an inclination to date.* So many times I have seen fellows spend weeks and months trying to get to know a girl well enough to try and determine if they could be interested in them. They are fearful of hurting them if they don't continue to date them, or they are afraid of getting hurt themselves when they are turned down. If we have the initial keen interest in a person to consider dating them--then we ought to get on with it immediately! We ought to use the dating period to become better acquainted, for that's the whole purpose of dating. We lose valuable time and pass up many great dating opportunities through vain fears. We also stop dating a person prematurely, fearing that we might be getting involved, and we don't want to hurt the person in case we need to stop later on. Some of those relationships could have grown into something wonderful if they had been given the chance.

DATING IS A GAMBLE!! Nothing ventured, nothing gained!! We need to ignore our fears, take the risk and venture into dating prospects with more optimistic hopes. We need to doubt less and "believe" more in the positive possibilities. If we are not interested in the person, we should stop dating them; but if we are uncertain and have no better prospects, we ought to give these kinds of relationships more time to grow.

The other extreme is that we fear cutting a long time relationship because *we don't want to hurt ourselves.* The author has personally known many couples that have literally dated for years, when they both felt nothing would come of it. They have had great times together, they have felt a lot of strong feelings for each other and they have had emotional dependance upon each other. Their own personal needs kept them going. Again, if you know that your relationship is on a "dead-end street," then have the courage to break it off and give both of you the chance to find something more meaningful.

TWO DATES MINIMUM: Some have the concept that you should never date a person just once, and that you have an "ethical responsibility" to date a person twice or else they will feel they are a terrible dud. There is a lot that can be said for the philosophy of trying to date a person at least two times. People can be so extremely different on a second date; they are more relaxed, they can be seen in a different kind of a dating situation, and they will appear so much more graceful and capable. Maybe they weren't feeling good the first time, or maybe your expectation level was exaggerated to the point that they couldn't help but be a great disappointment to you; whereas on the second date, your expectation level will be lower and you may find them to be quite impressive in ways you had not anticipated. However, there are times when the first date reveals so many areas where you are not compatible, that a second date is a waste of time for both of you. Again our key applies, *to date only those you really want to date!* Our questionnaires showed that very few really hold to the philosophy that you must date people twice, and there were some that wrote in specifically that they wouldn't want a person to date them a second time just because they felt they had to. Ask yourself the same question, and then work to implement **KEY 12: HAVE THE COURAGE TO DATE THOSE YOU REALLY WANT TO DATE!**

CREATING ROMANCE

PROBLEM 13: "HOW SOON DO I LET A PERSON KNOW THAT I LOVE THEM?"

We have written a great deal in this book about doing more and saying more to encourage a relationship. Most of us do not do enough most of the time. On the other hand, there are times when we overdo it. We are guilty of rushing a person before they are ready to be rushed. We let them know too soon how crazy we are about them and end up scaring them off. Both boys and girls are guilty of doing this.

I have talked with a lot of "popular" girls who have told me that if fellows let them know of their feelings too soon, it takes some of the challenge out of dating for the girls. It makes them feel like running the other way because they haven't determined yet how they feel. Secondly, they *want* to do a little bit of the pursuing and attracting. As one girl put it: "Women by nature are coy and conniving." She felt that it was partly because they weren't supposed to be the dominant individual and weren't expected to take the lead, so they sublimate with coyness and conniving to get their way. She illustrated the statement by relating how she would watch her little niece, who was very young, conniving to get something from her dad and was usually very successful, but her little brother couldn't begin to do the same thing. The roll of the females in our society seems to encourage a nature to scheme and connive for what they want and to be a little mischievous at times in the way they go about getting what they want. Men usually declare they hate it, but none the less they have been "trapped" by it through the ages. In the dating cycle it can be observed in the simple little ways in which women let men know that they like them. Actually, if a woman is too forthright and blunt with her feelings for a man, it can often make a man feel uncomfortably cornered, if he isn't sure of his own feelings.

The same type of game is played by the male in trying to win a lady, but it must never come out in feminine terms of coyness or conniving. These methods in their full application are repulsive to a woman to see in a man. Terms used to describe this "similar" phenomenon in men might be acting "cool" or "subtle." A man by nature is expected to be more open and direct. He is usually less complicated and easier to figure out. In our culture he is to lead out physically with a request for the date and with suggestions of where and what and when. He is more gruff in his voice, more dominant in stature, and typically more blunt in his manner than a woman. So a man has no reason to be "coy and conniving" and it is anything but masculine to be such. What a man should therefore be in the same psychological realm is "cool and subtle." *He knows what he thinks and feels about the girl, but he shouldn't wear his heart on his sleeve and tell her everything to begin with.* He would be wiser to retain his composure and hold back just enough to keep her curiosity up of what he really does think about her. Even as she begs and connives for his full emotional confession, he encourages her with small hints but retains his liberty to be free and uncommitted until the relationship has had plenty of time to grow.

Many women drop a man or can't decide to marry him because they really haven't chosen him; he has done all the asking and often the man is totally responsible for the relationship. The woman needs to reach a point where she is doing something to build the relationship also. She also needs to be emotionally reaching out for the man as much as the man is for the woman. Therefore, this is even more reason for a man not to open up his entire heart prematurely. If a girl knows she has a man wrapped around her little finger, she doesn't have to be sneaky or clever or work for the relationship, and it is likely that it will mean much less to her.

The argument is always presented: "But I don't want to play all the silly dating games of cat and rat." It isn't so much playing a game as it is realizing the psychological implications that things are only of worth when you have personally decided that you want them and have paid the price to get them. If one partner does everything for the relationship, the relationship has less chance of survival. You don't have to be dishonest, but you don't have to tell them every feeling you have for them until they have had an equal chance to decide their feelings and do something for the relationship. It is important to let a person know that you care for them and that you love them, *but in the proper time.* That timing will vary in every relationship, but the tendency is to move too fast once cupid has struck. Don't act bored. You can show genuine interest in a person and you can encourage them and let them know how much you are enjoying the date without committing your emotions to them.

GIVE ACCEPTANCE: Acceptance can be felt even on your first meeting and it can be felt in varying degrees as a relationship develops. The acceptance we eventually want is for another person to get to know us through and through, and after they know what we are really like, they still understand us and accept us for exactly what we are. Then and not till then can "LOVE" be given meaningfully. Before that point LOVE can only be given superficially, with little depth and lasting reward.

To conclude, then, there are important psychological aspects in dating for both sexes. Don't scare the other sex off with too much too soon of your emotional feelings. People don't want to feel trapped or cornered by your premature romantic confessions. Keep them to yourself until the timing is right. Give yourselves time to develop realistic awareness of each other. Give understanding and acceptance before demanding or giving too much emotional and committing love, then proceed slowly and cautiously. **KEY 13: PLAY IT COOL: BE ACCEPTING, BUT NOT OVERLY ANXIOUS!**

PROBLEM 14: "HOW CAN I SHOW MY ACCEPTANCE OF A PERSON?"

What we want more than anything else as individuals is to feel that we are *ACCEPTED* for what we are. Learning to fulfill this great human need will be indispensable in being successful in dating and especially when attempting to deepen the relationship. There are some things we cannot accept in certain people and we would be best to look for others to date. We should realize that no one is perfect and that no one person will be everything we dream of in a partner. Gentle encouragements in certain directions are always in order; but to attempt to renovate a person's entire personality, habits or convictions is a great mistake. If it doesn't destroy the relationship it will certainly hurt it. Conversely, the more acceptance we can radiate for a person, the greater are the chances of deepening that relationship and finding happiness with the person. Go out of your way to show an interest in their lives and in their activities. On the dates, make special efforts. For example, if you're bowling, watch them take their turn and be more concerned with their score than your own. We relate to people as we learn to accept them. Have an understanding and listening ear. You may not agree with what they say, but you don't have to create a disagreeable situation by making an issue out of things that don't really matter. Show approval as often as you can, compliment your date as often as you can, and learn to radiate from your eyes your acceptance of them. *LOVE springs forth from the seeds of acceptance.*

The following is a brief summary of some of the ways that a girl can show acceptance:

1. Be available for dates when he calls.
2. Show enthusiasm when you are asked for the date.
3. Thank the fellow for calling.
4. Greet him with a smile when he arrives for the date.
5. Take an interest in the fellow on the date, interest in his work or his projects.
6. Take the fellow by the arm when walking with him.

7. Dress and groom in such a way as to imply that the date means something to you.
8. Be on time for the date.
9. Sit relatively close to him if you're interested in him.
10. Be a good conversationalist.
11. Act as if you are enjoying the date and do your part to make it fun.
12. Invite the fellow in at the end of the date.
13. Thank him for the date.
14. Invite the fellow to dinner or to special events.

LITTLE ACTIONS OF ENCOURAGEMENT: We have already talked at length on how both the boy and girl can encourage each other in positive ways. We went into the communication of the eyes and face. Those little smiles and looks of approval are needed to encourage the relationship even before the first date. They increase in their importance if the relationship is going to really mean anything. Too many have been hurt in dating and they hesitate to show any real approval for fear of getting hurt again--but this is the risk you take every day of dating--you must learn to accept it.

EYE CONTACT: The art of giving these little smiles and looks of approval has to be learned. If they are given with too much encouragement, you may scare the poor person away. If they aren't given with enough emphasis, then they may not yield the desired results. You learn by trying! You will make many mistakes, but learn to accept your mistakes.

As you send out your little approving ovations, you will get feedback--they may have wanted to do the same, and the fact that you had the courage will make them feel more free to return the same little signs, grins, nods, and smiles. The language of "little motions" is interesting to observe and think about. The unspoken language often speaks louder than if there were attempts to verbalize our feelings. All this goes along with flirting. We have already talked about the importance of flirting. Your ability to flirt a little will go a long way in encouraging your date to be interested in you.

One simple suggestion to help in this area is to just look at the person a little more than you would usually do. *It's that eye contact that does it!* Have you ever noticed how little eye contact we have with strangers, and especially those of the opposite sex!? We never want to look right at the person. We try to look at them when they aren't looking our way. If our eyes should meet, we are quick to turn them away. This is just a trained and expected "norm" that we learn in our society. In some countries they do look right at each other for long periods of time with none of the embarrassment that we suffer here. Try it some time--look at your date for a good long interval--not constantly the whole date, but for one or two longer periods. Look deep into them and try to read their inner thoughts.

(The little scene of boy and girl happens many times where a fellow will watch a girl until she tells him not to look at her so much, because it embarrasses her. So the fellow stops giving her any notice for a few moments and then the girl tells him that she guesses she does like him watching her after all!)

This is the general idea, this is where the first little flutters of romance are felt. I have found myself all excited about a girl even before I knew her, just because of the way she looked at me. If I didn't like her, then of course it turned me off; but if I liked what I saw, it gave me the needed encouragement. To sum it up, it is these little unspoken glances that are needed to encourage your date and to deepen the relationship. **KEY 14: RADIATE ACCEPTANCE & CREATE ROMANCE!**

SECTION II

PHYSICAL ENCOURAGEMENTS

All the preceding suggestions on encouragement can be applied even without being very close to the person and without touching them. Probably one of the next steps in our exciting little venture is to get closer to the person. If you are in a car, girls can encourage the fellows by sitting just a little closer. Maybe you don't like to sit very close on the first date or the first few dates. But the point of this section is that if you want to encourage a fellow, you sit closer to him. It is a relative thing--some girls hang on the opposite door like their lives depended upon it, while others move right next to the fellow in the very beginning, and then there are the in betweens. Then of course, the bucket seats of the small sports car kind of predetermine the whole thing! Just as an idea, a girl might be wise to start a little closer to the door, and then if she likes the fellow she could move a little closer during the date or dates. But I'm sure most girls already have that idea figured out.

The same concept holds true wherever you are: walking, sitting elsewhere, or standing elsewhere. No matter where you are, you can encourage the person by being a little closer to them. Getting a little closer in your physical distance signifies that you are getting a little closer emotionally and romantically. If they move away, then keep your distance. Again, the concept is rather relative. Some nationalities stand closer to each other in normal conversation than others, some personalities do likewise. The real extrovert has a tendency to make an introvert feel very uneasy, because the extrovert will stand within inches, talking to them and breathing in their face, while the introvert is trying to put a little distance between them. But even though it is a relative thing, the concept still applies--*work with it and learn to adjust.*

WALKING WITH A PERSON: There is a lot communicated in the way you walk with each other. Does the fellow offer his arm for the girl to hold onto--especially in crossing streets or going into difficult areas? Girls look for this gesture from the fellow. It is not being forward, fellows, to offer your arm to a girl--it is common courtesy! Many girls will consider a fellow rude if he doesn't offer his arm. If the girl is reluctant to take your arm, it may indicate that she may be lacking some of the social grace and experience. And when you take a fellow's arm, girls--*TAKE HOLD OF IT!* Fellows are often annoyed when a girl just lingers there like a wet dishrag--

not really on and not really off. Take a semi-firm hold that shows you are there, but don't hang! There may be moments when a fellow helps the girl up a large step or something, but in general the arm is meant to be a *GUIDE,* to direct you where you are going. It has a real parallel to the dance floor.

DANCING: Some girls also make the mistake of "hanging" on a fellow on the dance floor. You may be little and light, but by the time he carries you twenty miles on the dance floor, he will never believe that you are as light as you may claim. Conversely, you don't dangle there like a wet fish--this is just as annoying! Take a fairly firm hold of your date, and then he can give you the signals of which way to turn. If you are limp, it is difficult to turn you, push or pull. *So remember the gentle, but firm holds!* Many girls are not aware of this concept at all, but if they had to be the fellow for a night and lug him around, they would soon catch on.

The same concept also applies to fellows. When a fellow takes hold of a girl to help them, girls like a firm but gentle grasp. They like the steady and strong feeling of a fellow. In fact, they are eager to feel your strength, *but not your brutality.*

LANGUAGE OF THE HANDS: In place of extending the arm to help a person, you may offer them your hand on occasions. It is interesting to see how soon she withdraws her hand. It tells you a good deal sometimes. As you want to deepen your relationship, the holding of hands can be a real fun part of it. Too many jump right on past it, and pass up one of the most vibrating and tingling experiences you can have--that is, of course, if the person means something to you.

A person's hands are one of the most sensitive areas of the body. You can feel what the person is really like, and you can often feel what they feel for you. Again, the firm but gentle hold, followed by the extra little squeeze of approval. The romance partly comes in the solid and firm feeling of the man's hand--which is like the rest of him. The girl's hand is soft and smooth and usually a little smaller--just like the rest of her. Fellows, if you want to deepen the relationship, reach for the girl's hand. Since "hand language" isn't verbal, there is nothing very committing about it all. If she is just limp, then she's probably noncommittal. If she is anxious to please you and encourage your continued friendship, she will probably communicate back to you. Again, it's just kind of "flirting" with each other, nothing too direct, but it all has its effect.

As with everything else we have mentioned, this again is relative. Maybe the girl just has something against holding hands. Maybe she isn't quite ready to commit herself even in the slightest little way, so she may pull back. Maybe she thinks you work too fast. Maybe she has the problem that many girls have--wet hands--and is worried about it, which makes her perspire all the more. (A little powder and carrying a hankie can help some.)

After a while, of course, holding hands can become rather routine. It can be overdone and lose its special affect for a while. Or maybe it just doesn't have the same effect on one of you. It may strike some funny, but work with it a little, experiment and see if you can learn the language of the hands.

KISSES

PROBLEM 15: "HOW SACRED IS A KISS?"

This depends on your culture and background. If you live in India, there is practically no dating because marriages are parentally arranged; therefore, kissing is taboo. There has been a recent controversy in India as to whether they should even permit kissing to be shown in their movies. One newspaper had headlines: "Kissing may lead to sexual anarchy."

It is possible that the philosophy of your parents may also be very structured against kissing in your courtship, and especially in your early dating. The author feels it would be difficult to prove that kissing is immoral or breaking any scriptural command. However, if your training is conservative and would restrain you from kissing in varying degrees, then you owe it to yourself to abide by your standards. And, you have a right to be respected by others for what your standards might be. I have had many friends who have only kissed the ones they have married. I have had other friends who have kissed only those that they felt very deeply for and hoped that their relationship would end in marriage. Then there are other friends who try to kiss as many as they can, as soon as possible.

AGE: The author doesn't wish to pass firm judgement in this area, but he would like to strongly encourage young daters to show restraint in their kissing. The idea of "sweet sixteen" is not a bad one! The author personally admires those who do wait for that ripe old age to arrive before giving away their kisses. Even after the age of sixteen, the author would encourage that *kisses be reserved for those that you feel something special for.* How special do they have to be? That is something that you must determine.

Kisses become significantly more important and meaningful as one arrives at the age and situation where marriage is desired and sought for. If you are a much older person and have sought marriage for many long years, and have also remained extremely conservative in not permitting anyone to kiss you, then it might be worthwhile considering a little less conservative approach. For it is in the kissing of an individual that you learn to develop a more involving relationship. You, in effect, risk emotional involvement with someone else. *It is in the sharing of love and matching of lips that often leads to the matching of lives.* But viewpoints always differ: some people don't take some things seriously enough, while others take some things too seriously. Kissing can be a lot of fun and very rewarding if you are sharing it with someone that you have hopes of building a deeper relationship with. In one discussion group held in preparation for this writing, a group of young people hashed back and forth the rightness and wrongness of kissing. After many opposing thoughts were considered, it appeared to be the general concensus of both the boys and girls that they did feel a little "wrong inside" if they had been kissing someone that didn't mean much to them, kissing for kissing's sake, or for the lust and physical stimulation. We might conclude then, that there must be something a little wrong about it, in such cases! It was brought out that kissing was most rewarding, and you felt excited and good inside, when your kisses were with someone that you felt a great deal of affection for.

LENGTH OF KISSING AT ANY ONE TIME: How long should you permit yourself to kiss someone? Again, this is something that has to be determined by you. The important thing is that you set up some standards for yourself of what you feel is right and then do everything in your power to stick by your standards. You know the limits of your own self-control.

More important than the exact length of time is the amount of lust that might be generated. Kissing has gone on far too long if it begins to stimulate a desire in either partner to go beyond kissing. If either of you feel you are tempted to have *intimate contact* with anything besides your two sets of lips, then you need to stop immediately! Every soul is born with the Spirit of Christ, and therefore has a conscience which tells him right from wrong. If you don't feel "good inside," then you know you have probably kissed far too long.

In general, then, remember the sacred nature of the kiss, and use **KEY 15: RESERVE KISSES FOR THOSE THAT YOU FEEL SOMETHING SPECIAL FOR!**

HOW DO I GET A KISS FROM A GIRL? Every fellow may have his own patented technique. Some just spring a kiss on a girl so fast that she doesn't know what happened. No leading up to it, and no warning. This might have its advantages, but it has several disadvantages as well. For one, you don't always know, when you are through, if she wanted it or not. And that's one of the nice things about a kiss--that both are in favor of it. Some girls don't want to be kissed by you or anyone else for a good while--this is their right and you should respect this.

If you want the kiss to be a little more special and romantic, if you want it to be kind of a mutual thing, *then you work up to it.* You move a little closer together and just enjoy that for a moment, then you may tenderly squeeze her hand for a moment or two. Next, you may rest your cheek on hers and just enjoy that for a brief period, and then comes the big moment! Now, was that so hard? Well yes, I guess it was. It is always easier said than done, and that is the very reason that makes a kiss exciting and special. There may be a little apprehension, a little wondering about how you will both respond. You wonder if you will like each others' kisses. You wonder if it will be exciting or rather dull. Some say that there's nothing like your first kiss--but that may depend on who kissed you. Maybe you have made kissing so common place that there is no thrill and nothing special. Let's hope not. Without trying to explain for ten pages *why,* it should be common sense not to kiss everyone. *Make them special!* If you don't like the person, don't kiss them or allow them to kiss you!! A kiss is kind of a committing thing--whether you want to admit it or not, it really is. It is intended to mean: "I Love You! I have special feelings for you. I am attracted to you. I am interested in our relationship and friendship."

Now, maybe you kiss everyone and it doesn't mean any of this to you. But remember that it does mean a great deal to some people, and you may hurt them emotionally if you flaunt your kisses and then move on to another girl. Keep them special and reserve them for those with whom you at least feel there might be some possibilities for a future. *When you become convinced that there is no future to your relationship, then you ought to stop kissing and stop dating!*

HOW CAN A GIRL GET A KISS? If a girl wants to be kissed, she pretty well needs to wait for the fellow. If she gives the first kiss, she risks scaring the fellow away because of her forwardness, and because he wasn't ready and would prefer to call the shots. However, a girl can do many things to encourage a kiss. She can start by watching her grooming and general appearance. *When a girl looks pretty enough to kiss, she is much more likely to be kissed.* She can take pains to make sure she has no bad body odors and can wear a moderate amount of perfume. She can be sure that she has brushed her teeth and that she doesn't have bad breath. Using mouth wash and always carrying some breath mints can help insure that your mouth doesn't have the "kiss of death." (These last suggestions would also apply to the man.) She can then be romantic at every opportunity. If they are holding hands, she can squeeze his hand a little. If they are looking at each other, she can give inviting smiles. Romance is made by reaffirming to each other that you are interested. One person smiles, and the other smiles back with even more emphasis, and each act becomes a little more encouraging and reassuring. She can also move a little closer to her fellow and be in a convenient position to get caught. Putting your head on his shoulder can be one of the most potent suggestions. But the author would guess that girls don't need too many suggestions, because they already have these things figured out.

HOW MANY DATES BEFORE KISSING? Our questionnaires revealed that the most common date for kissing a person for the first time is on the "third date." There were many who kissed on first and second dates, and some a few dates thereafter, but there were far more that received their first kiss on the third date than any other time. This may surprise many people and maybe even shock a few, to think that people will kiss that early in a relationship. But really, it isn't too amazing when you consider what makes things *romantic.* The newness of the situation, the unknowns about the person, the great hopes that may still be there that this might be the person you have been waiting for all your life. After you have had a great number of dates with one person, you begin to accept the person more for what you know of them, and it is really a less likely time to begin to kiss, when the person seems a little more "human" and down-to-earth. Some of the initial excitement is worn off and the romance has subsided to some degree.

There is another factor that influences kissing by the third date also. It is illustrated by the response of one girl to a questionnaire. We asked the question: "About how many of the fellows you date kiss you by the third date?" and she was one of the girls that responded: "100 percent!" How shocking? It may be to some. But her answer was interesting. She said that the reason that 100 percent of the fellows she had dated had kissed her by the third date was because if she didn't really like them a great deal, she would never go out with them a third time. So in her dating pattern she would cut them off before that, and this increased the number on the third date who would kiss her!

It is this idea that explains why so many do kiss those that they have dated very little. You date a person because you are excited about them to begin with--or at least the fellows are--and they are the ones that lead out. It is quite common for fellows to say that they don't date a girl unless they are very attracted to her. They wouldn't date a girl unless they felt like they would enjoy kissing her. That being the case, it isn't really too unusual that people kiss at such an early period in a dating cycle. It is on their minds, they feel romantic about the person, they are emotionally anxious about their feelings, and if they are given half the chance to express them, they do so.

I'm not advocating that people should kiss by the third date!! But I am explaining what some of the "norms" are--what is common in the dating world. And whatever your feelings might be toward the subject, it would be helpful and meaningful for you to realize what others are doing and expecting as you date them. There is no law, there are many who have their own private patterns and do wonderfully with them. If you are a girl and don't want a fellow to advance toward you to kiss you--then don't allow too much romance to get started, and don't encourage it.

HOW DOES A GIRL TURN A KISS DOWN? One of the difficulties is that fellows aren't going to ask you if they can kiss you--or at least they shouldn't. There was one question in our questionnaires that all girls were 100 percent agreed upon, and that was, *they didn't want a fellow to ask them if they could kiss them, they wanted them to just do it!*

Therefore, as a fellow just tries to "do it," what is a girl to do if she doesn't want the fellow to kiss her? She has about four possibilities:

1. She can let him whether she wants him to or not.

2. She can turn her head, but stay in range so that he kisses her on the cheek instead of on the lips. This is usually considered as less than a real kiss by both parties.

3. She can sometimes back away quickly and avoid it.

4. If he tries again, she can politely say: "Thanks Bill, but I'd rather not be kissed just now."

In the questionnaires, most fellows indicated they didn't mind getting turned down for a kiss at first, and that they would keep dating the girl. However, they indicated in later questions that they expected to be able to kiss her at some time not too far distant, or else they would feel there was no future to their relationship.

Realizing that some fellows feel this way, if you have set your standards of "no kissing," you'd better explain your ideals to the fellow if you have any hopes in wanting that particular relationship to continue. Many fellows who expect kisses will readjust their expectation levels while dating you.

SECTION III

DEEPER INVOLVEMENT & SMALLER COMMITMENTS

5% MORE PRODUCES 300% MORE RESULTS

In an earlier chapter we introduced the concept of how a girl could make herself more successful in getting dates if she would do more herself. This concept also applies to the area of deepening a relationship. Be 5 percent more progressive in being available, in suggesting fun activities, in inviting him to dinner and special activities, and in doing little special things for your man. Your results will be outstanding! But beware not to overdo your promotion--5 percent is not 50 percent more on your part. A man does not want to feel he is being cornered or that the woman is taking over the leadership. Some girls dominate too much, once they get a man dating them, and they need to *reduce* their promotion by 50 percent. But the average girl doesn't do enough to encourage the relationship and would be 300 percent more successful in deepening a relationship if she would take 5 percent more initiative in promoting the relationship.

PROBLEM 16: "WHAT ELSE CAN I DO TO DEEPEN A RELATIONSHIP?"

SPONTANEITY: To make a relationship more meaningful, there must be more spontaneity both in getting dates and in the dating activities, as was mentioned in a previous chapter. I remember one outstanding girl I dated that I had to call at least 10 days ahead and give in detail what the date was going to involve. I believe we were both interested in each other, but the rigidity and formal structure prevented the deepening of our relationship. On the other hand, one of the most meaningful relationships I ever had was with a girl that I originally didn't plan on dating extensively. Our friendship grew because it was so easy to just drop in at her apartment and so comfortable to just visit with her with nothing specifically planned.

Because of so many variable factors, the ideal spontaneity is not always accomplishable, but it can be worked towards. The ideal is to be able to just drop in occasionally and enjoy visiting. The ideal is to be able to call on the spare of the moment and get a date that will begin in a few minutes. *A fellow should not take this approach constantly,* or the girl will resent it and feel she is being taken too much for granted. Plan some of the dates further in advance and with a little more formality. Then use the spontaneous dating approach as an extra. Both fellows and girls need to be less formal if their dating is to be meaningful. Dating needs to develop to the point where you are like too small kids in a neighborhood, and the boy comes over to ask if you can come out and play. In fact, the author has used those very words on a couple of surprise visits, with pleasing results.

INVITE THE MAN IN: To increase the spontaneous atmosphere of dating, a girl needs to invite her date into her home or apartment when it is possible and won't disturb her roommates or parents. When you haven't had time to visit in the car or elsewhere, it does so much for the date. It lets the fellow know that you are anxious to be with him longer. It gives you a chance to visit and get to know each other so much better. So often you have rushed to the show house and then you rush back and you have done nothing to build a relationship.

This is one of those appropriate times when a girl can do 5 percent more. If you don't like the date, don't invite him in, but if you do--bake some cookies or a cake, and maybe have some ice cream conveniently available. Clear the potential plan with parents or roommates and then tell the fellow that you just baked some cookies today and he must sample them for you. Some girls do it all the time and some never do it. The author's observation is that girls become more popular and have more lasting relationships with boys when they invite them in. Fellows would do well to accept the invitation when and if it comes, and if you know the girl well enough, under the right conditions you might even suggest the idea yourself. Meaningful relationships are not developed on the formal structured dates, but in relaxed and spontaneous activities.

BECOME A PART OF THE FAMILY: You should try to get to know something about each other's background and get to know the other's family in whatever ways possible. You can learn a surprising amount about a person just by watching their family. You may be able to understand some of their habits better, and it will surprise you to see some of the same mannerisms in other members of the family that you have seen in your date. You will understand better why they think and feel the way they do. Some say that if you want to know what your wife-to-be is going to become, take a good look at her mother. And for the girls--take a look at the boy's father. There will be changes, there will be exceptions, but there may be striking predictive powers in this simple little observation. Watch the little brothers and sisters and you might get a good idea of what they might have been like while growing up. Observe how your date respects their parents, for they will tend to respect their marriage partner much the same. Also they will tend to view the roles of husband and wife as they have observed them in their own home.

Too many daters avoid the family like it was some necessary evil to be ignored as much as possible. Not only is it a great place to learn to know the other person, but it should be a place in which you feel comfortable. Hopefully you are not going to ask your date to never see their family again if you should marry them. During the dating period they may want to get away from them more often than not, but after marriage they will want to return home often. Some daters say in ignorance: "Well, I'm not marrying the family!" *But you really are marrying the family more than you realize,* and it is important that you can feel somewhat a part of the new family you are marrying into. Not everything needs to seem natural, there will always be some unnatural aspects to it, but if you don't blend into the family at all, then chances are that you don't blend into the life of your date as much as you think you do.

The importance of this concept never seemed all that important to me in my first few years of dating, but I became more and more aware of its importance as I dated various girls and tried to feel natural with their families. There was one experience in particular which brought it to my attention. It was in a conversation with one of my good friends. I had met him at college and therefore knew nothing of his background. All I knew was that he was an outstanding person, very impressive in nearly every way. He was very pleasant to be with, very religious, very honest, and had the highest of standards. One day I was in his room talking to him, and he startled me a little by saying: "John, you don't know how lucky you are to have the outstanding family you do. Your father is known by many for his positions and his high integrity. You see, I don't have anything like that." I stopped him to assure him that he must have a good family also. But he corrected me by saying that there was nothing impressive about his family whatsoever. Then he related a long discouraging history of his family. I don't remember all the details exactly, but his father had served two prison terms, two of his brothers had been in prison, and he had another brother who was in a detention home. He had sisters who became pregnant and were forced into "shotgun" marriages. His whole family history was one continuous cycle of thievery and being in trouble with the law. None of them had much education, they were poor and lived in a sad environment.

His life had been changed by going away to school and getting in with the right group. He became very religious and even went on a mission overseas for his church. His life was completely different from that of his family. Then he asked: "Now how do I tell all of this to a girl?" I responded with the typical immature statement, that she wasn't "marrying his family." But he cut me short by saying: "Yes, but I love my family! And I want to visit them often. Now, I need a girl that can adjust to that type of situation, but at the same time be altogether different from what they are. Now how many girls are going to feel comfortable around my family like they would around your family?"

I then began to appreciate more of what a blessing I did have, because this was one additional dating problem this good fellow was always conscious of and concerned about. I also learned more forcefully that you do marry into the family situation and that you can't expect your mate to give up her family entirely. Your family becomes hers, and her family becomes yours in a very real sense. If they are many miles apart from you it may become less of a problem--but it is still a potential joy or problem. So, look the family over and size them up just as you do your dates.

MORE THAN WEEKEND DATING: Many girls and fellows get so busy in their work or in school studies that they start limiting their dating activity to just weekends. This is fine and dandy for the success of your studies or your work, but count out much success in the dating area. Meaningful relationships are nearly always developed with more than weekend contact. Maybe your time is limited, but you can make dates just short visits--just 30 or 60 minutes at the end of the day. You will study harder and accomplish more if you know you are working for that break. You could take a short walk and talk, or get a root beer. Maybe you could play a small game of Table Tennis or some other game. Maybe you could have a study date in the library where you honestly study! Everyone has to eat, so get together for lunch or dinner. Do anything you have to, but if you are seriously desirous of deepening a relationship, you need to consider working in more than just weekend dating.

In all my dating experience I have found that those girls I wasn't able to date more than once a week were the ones that I could never develop anything with, of real depth. Those who were really interested in me seemed to have the time to see me. Usually they had all the time in the world for me, and if they didn't have, they rearranged their schedules so they could work me in, or they made alternative suggestions that worked out just as well.

Some girls get themselves so tied up in activities that they really don't have time for dating. They belong to a dozen clubs, service and social units etc., and they just don't have one evening that they can give a fellow for a date. While it is great that they are out mixing in these groups, they ought to try to keep themselves open once in a while for dating opportunities that might come along. Whether girls like their position or not, it is one of taking what fellows have to offer, when they offer it.

It is a wise girl that tries to put first things first. If a fellow comes along that she is interested in--she breaks her other plans of going to the ladies' sewing bee, or singing in the church choir, or maybe skipping her social unit for that night. Some things you can't get out of, but there are many that you can. *Girls, in order to be successful in your dating, you need to be very flexible and willing to sacrifice!* You need to be able to adjust your plans and work them in with what the fellow has planned. You need to be *available!* Some girls are so busy in doing secondary things that in all seriousness they are *not available* to have a meaningful relationship with a fellow. Keep busy girls, but keep busy in things that can be alternated and changed for your dating situations. If the most preferred man on campus called you, and you had a crush on him, you'd probably be willing to get thrown out of some of your clubs for a chance to go with him. Well, maybe the fellow that has just called isn't the most preferred man, but if he shows any promise, treat him as such, and he may indeed become such for you.

FELLOWS: Sometimes we get in a rut of just dating on the weekends, and we are a little afraid of asking a girl even twice in the same week for fear that she will think that we are overly anxious about her etc. Well, there are times when you don't want to rush a girl too fast and too much at first; however, if you are eventually going to develop a meaningful relationship with them, you will need to be seeing a lot of them. Many of my most successful relationships have come on fast. You get the first date and on the first date you may arrange for a date on the very next day--not waiting for the next weekend at all. You follow that date up with maybe one the very next day, and then at the same time, say that you'd like to reserve a date for that weekend as well. If they like you--they'll love it!! If they don't like you, no harm done--all you have done is to find out a bit sooner, and you have saved everybody a lot of time.

An example of some "concentrated time together" happened to a friend of mine. He was extremely busy with long hours on a job, combined with pushing to get a Master's Program finished at school. He had dated this one young lady a fair amount, but had essentially dropped her for a while with no special feeling for action. Then he caught the flu so bad that he had to stop working and stay at home for a while. His girl was also sick enough to miss work, and so they kept each other company in their misery. He wasn't able to study, so they did a lot of talking and visiting, and suddenly he realized how much she really meant to him. He wonders now if he would have ever become engaged if it hadn't been for that sickness. Just another success example of really concentrating on a relationship to the exclusion of everything else!

ROMANTIC SUMMER: I remember a Summer School I attended once. My date was only in the state and on the campus for about two months, so I knew we had to work fast if there was going to be anything to our relationship. I also knew that she was very popular; in fact, I was going around with about five fellows who were all verbally talking about dating her. I didn't say much--I just went and got the date. The first date was so great that I asked her to about three different things the very next week. Then jokingly I said: "My, I guess I've really booked you up haven't I?" She just laughed and said, "You don't see me complaining do you?" She wasn't either--we had something great going. I was floating around on one of the highest clouds I'd ever ridden in my life up to that time. Before those dates had concluded I had her booked up heavily again. Now the point is, if I'd followed the traditional approach: wait until your second date to ask her for another date in advance, I wouldn't have gotten anywhere. Other fellows would have moved in and taken things over before I could have asked, and she wasn't going to wait around all summer just for me to ask for a date once a week. I had the courage to ask and it paid off wonderfully. It was one of the most romantic summers of my life!

FIND A PROJECT: Attempt to have dating activities that are mutually involving. Start a hobby and work on it together. Start some project together that produces something meaningful. As an author I have had some very enjoyable times working on the books I was writing with a date. We have also worked together in producing them physically in various printing steps. Several dates have told me how meaningful they felt these dates were, and how they felt that so many other dates they had had were lacking in meaningfulness.

One wise man was talking to a group of young men returning to America after being gone for two years. He asked them how they planned to find a wife. After listening to their ideas for a while, he told them to *find someone that they liked and that looked like a real good prospect, and then go out of their way to ask that person to do something for them.*

This advice has a lot of good in it, if used properly. It is good for both men and women to experiment with, but especially meaningful for the men to experiment with, because a woman's life is more oriented to one of devotion to the home, family and husband. The husband directs his interest in the business world and outside of the home, and much of his work is done indirectly for the woman, while a woman's service is more direct. *A relationship becomes meaningful when you actually become involved in each other's lives*--when you start helping one another do the things that make up your life. You share each other's families, each other's projects, each other's convictions and goals. Don't be reluctant to ask individuals you are dating a great deal to do things for you. See how they respond to your request. It is significant and important as you consider committing yourselves to each other. **KEY 16: INVITE YOUR COMPANION INTO YOUR LIFE!**

COMMITMENT STAGES

PROBLEM 17: "HOW DO I DEVELOP COMMITMENTS?"

DEFINITION OF TERMS: The various stages of commitments in the dating cycle are called by numerous names. They vary among different geographical locations and from generation to generation. It isn't important what they are called, but for purposes of understanding we will define four stages of Commitment as: Going Steadily, Going Steady, Getting Pinned, and Becoming Engaged.

1. *Going Steadily:*
   This is where you date one person a great deal and do very little dating with others and maybe none at all. You have no verbal commitment, but you are both counting on each other to some extent.
2. *Going Steady:*
   This is where you are only dating one person and you have verbally agreed not to date anyone else.
3. *Getting Pinned:*
   This is the stage where you are only dating one person and have verbally agreed not to date anyone else and the girl has agreed to accept and wear a boy's pin, friendship ring, his sweater or something as a token of the agreement. You may have even both exchanged something as a token of

your agreement not to date others. Customs vary and you may have created your own symbolism.

4. *Becoming Engaged:*
   This is the stage where you have agreed to become married and will therefore not date others. The girl may have received a ring or some other token to symbolize their verbal agreement.

COMMITMENTS FOR YOUNG DATERS: The paradox of the dating cycles is that very young daters don't seem to find it difficult at all to find someone they can get serious with and want to get too serious right away. Then, there are the "old maids" and "old bachelors" who can't seem to find anyone to date at all, at least no one that they can get serious with and make commitments. Both would be far better off if they could exchange places. Young people shouldn't limit themselves to one person, they should date many and learn to have fun with a lot of different personalities. But it is more easily spoken than practiced. Young daters are just as anxious to find someone very special as anyone. And it is always easier to call back someone that has already accepted a date than it is to branch out and start all over.

Author's experience in High School: He remembers very well being very excited about a young lady in high school. There were many friends getting pinned at school, so I decided that I was ready to do the same. I proudly announced my intentions at the breakfast table, not asking, but telling them what I intended to do. To my surprise, my parents spoke up and said the following: "Well that's fine, if that's what you really want, but we as your parents would recommend that you don't." I was defiant and angry that they would tell me this. I demanded to know what the difference was, we weren't really going with anyone else anyway. They just simply replied: "Well, what's the difference then?"

The very fact that I was wanting to do it made it obvious that I knew there was a difference. I knew that making a "formal commitment" made it much more special and I felt it would be more exciting. I wanted to do it rather badly, but my parents never asked me to do a great deal, so when they even suggested what they would "rather," I was stuck. Well, it turned out to be a blessing. They feared that there might be an early marriage right out of high school, before I could get into college and do some other important things. I seriously doubt that this would have happened to me, but it did happen to many others at the same school. We continued our relationship in a "steadily" fashion for a few years, but we also dated a few others and gained some interesting insights into other personalities.

I wouldn't have admitted it then, but looking back now I realize that I didn't know that much about dating. And because I hadn't dated a large number of other girls, I really didn't know that much about the girl I was dating--simply because I didn't have enough to compare her with. I was lucky to have found a pretty wonderful girl, but it would have still benefited both of us to have done more dating with others than we did. Briefly stated, then, *DATE AS MANY AS YOU ARE ABLE IN YOUR EARLY DATING EXPERIENCE.* This will give you great comparative powers that can be obtained in no other way.

COMMITMENTS FOR SERIOUS DATERS: Assuming that you have the experience and that you are now anxious to develop some relationships that will result in marriage in the near future, then it is important that you center your attention on a few special individuals and eventually start going steadily with just one person.

HOW LONG BEFORE COMMITMENTS SHOULD BE MADE? There is no time period. Your author knows of older couples who were talking marriage on the first date and became very happily married not many months later. The "right" time is an emotional element. It depends on your age, your interest and love for each other, how well you have gotten to know each other, and how well you fulfill each other's needs and personalities. Many date for years and are not ready for commitment stages, while others make commitments very successfully after the first few dates. Some couples progress so rapidly that they don't need intermediate steps in becoming engaged. However, most couples require more time and the progressive steps can be of great help to them.

A verbal commitment to go steady can be helpful to a girl, because she can then have a good solid reason to turn other fellows down and concentrate on the one she feels the most toward. Likewise, it is helpful to a fellow in that he doesn't have to feel frustration and mixed emotions when he has to compete for time with his favorite girl. Some couples have even approached going steady on a trial basis, for a specified period of time. One suggested that they try it for three weeks during a special Christmas season.

Going steady can be beneficial to both in testing out their own feelings while not being able to date others. Some learn that their date means more than ever to them, while others may realize that their "steady date" isn't all they thought they were, now that they can see them in more concentrated light of constant company. People's personalities change when they are under commitments. They may let down too much and take you for granted, or they may become far too demanding in what they expect of you. The simple prelude of going steady can foretell what it would be like to be engaged and even give a few insights of what marriage might be like.

Many fellows may desire an engagement, but they prefer to ask a girl to go steady first and to become pinned just as some assurance of not getting turned down. It would hurt a great deal more to be turned down on a marriage proposal than it would for going steady.

Wisdom would certainly dictate the advantages of using all the preliminary stages you can in dating, to assure both of you that the other person is the one you really want. Trial stages of commitment can be protective and most helpful in preparing a couple for the more serious commitments.

KEY 17: DEVELOP COMMITMENTS BY STAGES!

Chapter 4

HOW DO YOU KNOW WHEN YOU SHOULD GET MARRIED?

It may not seem like much of an answer, but really, the only intelligent answer possible is: get married *WHEN YOU FEEL RIGHT ABOUT IT!* We will go into other ideas and specifics that will help solve this problem, but it still boils down to the "rightness of feeling!"

YOU'LL KNOW: If you ask the "old marrieds," they will often answer with something like the following: "You'll know!" You'll know what? What are you supposed to feel, what is it like? Everyone has their own private experience, and there are many who never have any doubts or wonders and just know without question that they have found the right person. On the other hand, there are great numbers of people who have questions right up to and even after the ceremony. The author was talking to his father who has performed literally hundreds upon hundreds of marriages, and he indicated that it is surprising how many brides don't go through with the marriage plans right at the last moment, just before the ceremony is to begin, and they will not show up. Can you imagine the problems that situation could cause for so many people? The point here is that many do greatly struggle with doubts and questions before marriage as to whether they are doing the right thing. Sometimes the memories of other love affairs come back to haunt them, and they wonder which one it is that they really love the most. They wonder if they are really experiencing all of the feelings they are supposed to have, or if they might find someone else they could love even more. Many get married on the love that their companions have for them, and they have very little understanding of how they themselves really feel. What will the *future,* that great unknown, hold for them?

WHY DO PEOPLE GET MARRIED?

People get married for a long list of reasons. It is usually a combination of many reasons, but there is often one dominant reason above the others. Some of these are:

1. *Love:*
   They love each other, or one loves the other sufficient to convince the other.
2. *Companionship:*
   They are lonely and want someone to share their lives with, and may pick the most likely individual without total regard to their degree of love or commitment.
3. *Outside pressures:*
   In many cultures the parents pick the marriage companions and even in this culture where it isn't customary, some children will yield to the persuasion of parents or friends, that a certain person is right for them. Also, many yield to social pressures, such as: "Others are getting married," and "It seems the thing to do."
4. *Security:*
   Many women don't want to work and feel insecure even when working, and the thought of someone to protect and provide for them is a strong driving force to convince them that marriage is desirable. Many men also want the security of someone to take over where their mothers left off and provide a warm atmosphere to call "home."
5. *Status:*
   Many marry for the great wealth that the other might have or will inherit. Or maybe the person or their family is famous, which will provide great status.
6. *Intellectual decision:*
   There may not be a warm love for the person, but in-

telligence tells them that they will be capturing a great prize.

7. *Beauty and Sex:*
   Love at first sight, they marry for the beautiful or handsome features of their partner. They may feel that the urge to enjoy sexual freedom is so strong that they can't live without them, irregardless of what else the person may be.
8. *Personality and Intrigue:*
   The individual has personality plus, they may be the "life of the party," witty and funny. They may be very captivating and create a great intrigue and curiosity which stimulates great desire to marry the person.
9. *Escape:*
   They feel dominated by parents or their present surroundings, and may be looking for someone to marry so that they can escape into a new world.
10. *Spiritual Convictions:*
   They may have studied their feelings of love and sought the help of their Father in Heaven, and feel that He has answered their prayers that this is the right person for them.

There are many other reasons, but the above are some of the most common reasons that compel individuals into marriage. So, if you are attempting to decide if you are ready for marriage, you might compare your reasons with some of these and attempt to decide if your reasons are sound and good. There are too many that marry for the wrong reasons or at least for weak reasons. There ought to be a combination of many good reasons to justify a marriage.

Going back to the idea that so many people give you that "you'll know" when it's the right person, the author would suggest again that *many don't know!* And there have been times when the writer felt he knew, but later on he was so grateful that he really didn't know after all.

The author will now suggest three major areas that an individual ought to consider in helping them decide if they have found an individual that is right for them:

FEEL RIGHT IN THREE MAJOR AREAS AT LEAST:

1. Feel right about your emotional feelings of love.
2. Feel right about your reasoning and intellectual feelings.
3. Feel a spiritual rightness about the relationship.

Going through the above process might be termed confirming or obtaining a "confirmation"; you assure yourself that you feel right in the areas of Emotional, Intellectual, and Spiritual Love.

EMOTIONAL CONFIRMATION: We already have an entire chapter on the subject of love and don't intend repeating it here. Suffice to say, if you are having extreme doubts as to your love for the person, then it must not be love. When you are in love with the person, you are anxious to be with them and do things for them. You feel an emotional commitment towards them. You may feel some real emotions of love for other people also, but marriageable love is when you are willing to place any emotions for others aside and give your full emotional commitment to the one you plan to marry.

INTELLECTUAL CONFIRMATION: Attempt to put the emotional feelings of love for the other person aside. Try to stand back and look at the individual as if you were an outside party looking into the relationship. Gather all the data that you can. Are you impressed with the person when they are in the company of others? Do you have similar backgrounds of culture, education, and interests? Do you have the same kinds of goals and can you work on things together? Do you have the same religious and ethical standards? Ask your close friends to be frank and honest in telling you what they think of the person you are dating and how they match you.

The author often double dates with fellows that have sharp opinions, and those poor girls never know the going over they get at the end of the date. I have a close friend who doubles with his brother and sisters who are all close in age. They have a very tight bond in their family unit and really enjoy being with each other. He told me that he could always tell when he was with the wrong type of girl, not because of his own ability to judge sometimes, and not because of what his kin would say, but he could just feel how impressed they were. Either his date just didn't fit into the family circle or else she did. Well, most of us aren't big enough to take much advice from family members and especially from mother and dad, and yet maybe their advice and evaluation can't be beat!

Do all of the parts fit together? Make a list of your personality traits, your goals and aspirations, and seriously ask yourself how well they may help you achieve them. Find out what their list entails and ask yourself honestly how well you will help them fulfill their aspirations. We don't necessarily have to have all the same goals and personality traits, but we should compliment each other. For example, if you have a very quick temper, for your sake you'd better try to find someone that will not respond in the same way at the same time. There are many other complimenting situations that might be desirable. But we should not confuse *complimentary* traits and goals with *conflicting* traits and goals.

SPIRITUAL CONFIRMATION: You are probably aware of the fact by now that this author believes in a divine being. He feels no hesitancy in acknowledging this belief; in fact, he is anxious to voice his convictions. He knows that God lives and that He answers prayers and helps men in their lives! It is unfortunate for individuals who have important decisions to feel they cannot seek God's help! Millions have been intelligent enough to seek His help and have been richly rewarded. So humble yourself, kneel down and ask your God to help you make the right decisions. Use any home-spun phrases you choose, but talk to Him as you would anyone that you revere.

Don't demand an answer, but request an answer. Don't make up your mind what the answer is going to be, but be open to new ideas. Be prepared to accept that the answer might be NO! Don't pray for just what you think is selfishly best for you, but best for all concerned. Don't plead for the answer with so much frenzy that you work yourself into agonizing anguish, but ask with simple faith believing that He will help you. Don't set a time limit, but request an answer in the due time of the Lord. Don't ask for angels or voices, but ask for a sensitive mind and spirit to detect His inspiration and impressions. Don't ask Him to stop you if it is wrong, but ask Him to guide you in the decisions you contemplate. Don't ask Him to make the total decision, for He gave you the free agency to do that yourself, but ask Him to guide and direct your thoughts and to give verification of the decisions that you tentatively select. Don't seek a bolt of lightning, but seek a peace of mind and a serene assurance in your final decisions. Live worthy to receive answers, and when you receive your answers, take no credit yourself, but always give your Father in Heaven the credit and glory.

The following verse has been one of the author's favorites:

I know not by what method rare,
But this much I know that God answers prayer.

I know not if the blessing sought
Will come in just the way I thought.

But leave my prayers with him alone,
Whose will is wiser than my own.

Assured that he will grant my request
Or send some answer far more blessed.

How could a person write a chapter on how to decide about marriage without bringing in prayer? If you don't believe, just try to believe a little bit and give God a chance to help you. If you can do nothing more, start with simple meditation and thinking upon your creator and feel after the "peace" that He brings to so many troubled hearts.

MEDITATION: Whether you believe in God or not, it is important to spend some time meditating with your "self." Many who believe in God will spend time praying, but will jump up and forget to meditate. This is unfortunate, because it is during the meditation that God will often speak back to you; and He speaks with impressions and thoughts and He can direct your thoughts to the answers.

In addition, you can learn much from meditation. Everyone needs to just think and meditate on worthwhile things. Turn off the TV, get by yourself and direct your mind to think into positive areas. You might think about the purpose of your existence, what you can create in the world, or what service you can render for others that would be worthwhile.

If it is a problem that you want to solve, never spend too long meditating on it at any given time. You are probably already thinking about it too much. After giving a problem a certain amount of deep concentration, turn your mind off of it and involve yourself in thoughts of a completely different nature. Allow your subconscious mind to work on the problem and it will provide you with the answer with far greater speed than you can imagine, whereas continuous thought will only confuse the issue more. To those who have learned the art of meditation, life becomes more rich and successful, more peaceful and rewarding.

And so it is with making decisions on who you should marry. *Use all of the sources available to you. Listen to others, listen to the Lord, and listen to your own mind through intervals of meditation.*

MARRIAGE DECISIONS BY WAY OF THE SUBCONSCIOUS MIND

The author has one of his college degrees in Psychology, and he has found in his studies that it is quite common for psychologists to explain a great deal of "hard-to-explain decisions and behavior" by means of the subconscious mind. It is extremely difficult to explain how most people finally make their decision to get married. Many people have various answers to give, but when you really pin them down, they aren't quite sure how they really made the final decision.

It is very possible that some psychologists are right, in many cases, in stating that marriage decisions are made in the subconscious mind. But it is difficult to prove this because the subconscious mind is also referred to as the "unconscious mind": the mind that takes over in our sleep and maybe other times when we are unaware of its activity. However, we become aware of the results of its activity when we find that we wake up with the answers to many of the problems we might be trying to solve in school, work or life. Many people wake up in the middle of the night and write down ideas that appear to flash upon them. This happened to Francis Scott Key, who produced the "Star Spangled Banner." Then there are others who can take a problem to bed and wake up in the morning with the solution to their problem.

If the reader can accept the above concepts, it should also sound reasonable that many solve their marriage questions in their subconscious mind. But since the process of input and output of the subconscious mind is so mysteriously difficult to understand, the usefulness of this knowledge seems to have limited value to many. However, to some it can be helpful when they understand some of the possible correlations. To explain further, many psychologists believe that a person subconsciously seeks out a person whose personality is the compliment of his own. Those areas in which he might personally be weak or lacking are sought for in a companion subconsciously. We may not always be aware or conscious that we are seeking these complimentary qualities, but our subconscious minds stimulate us into feeling a curiosity and desire for some talented person who possesses some of the personality traits we feel lacking in our personality. And they may hopefully find in us some areas, felt by this silent "sixth sense," which are superior to them. This mysterious attraction process is labeled "LOVE."

Their strong points joined to our weak points relieve the tensions and stresses created out of our feelings of inadequacies. We often feel frustrated and unable to compete with others simply because of some small facets in our personality which cause us to feel inferior. It doesn't matter who the individual is, how brilliant and accomplished they may be in many areas, there are still small areas of weakness in their personality.

We are all the superior of everyone else in some small ways, and we are likewise inferior to everyone else in some other small ways, so we unconsciously seek out company that can both accept us and compliment our weaknesses. As we find potential partners that don't compete with us in our weak areas, we feel relieved and fulfilled! As human beings we all hunger for this matching fulfillment. The release of the tensions and the feeling that with them we are a complete human being is greatly rewarding--and this emotional fulfillment we also call "LOVE!"

Some feel this means we should look for our opposites, but this is not true. We will find enough opposite characteristics even after marrying our twin. We should match as close as we can in interests and backgrounds; but personality-wise, *we need to find our compliment*--not our contrasts, nor our opposite, but our compliment. A man who wants to be boss will do poorly to marry a woman with the same obvious drive. One of the major reasons for marital problems is that couples are often two personalities with the same complex unconscious needs, and they do not help each other in fulfilling them.

In conclusion, we will be more successful in dating and marriage if we can learn to recognize our deeper emotional needs, our subconscious needs and weaknesses, and find someone who fulfills them.

HOW DO YOU BECOME ENGAGED?

Assuming that you have worked out the problems of deciding whether or not you should marry a person, then we can move on to the delightful moment of becoming engaged. Every fellow has some of his own private ideas as to where and how he is going to propose to the young lady. There is usually some special wording or manner, or some special place in which he hopes to surprise the girl. It may seem corny to someone else, but some individualism and originality at this moment is most desirable to make it even more romantic!

SECRETLY AT FIRST: The traditional method of becoming engaged is to run out and announce it to the world that very night or the next day. This usually works out for most people, but there are a few that find themselves under undue pressure from other people. Others want to know when the marriage date is going to be and all the details. They don't mean any harm, but often a couple wants a little time to make many of these decisions. Others want to know how it happened and just how they feel about each other. Very often both the fellow and girl have some second thoughts right after getting engaged and this kind of undue pressure can really cause difficulties. One method of solving this problem is to have a "silent period" when you become engaged but you don't tell anyone else. It may last for a couple of weeks or a month or even longer. It gives a couple a chance to enjoy their new commitment to each other that can be experienced in no other way. If there is any hesitancy on the part of either person, they can analyze their feelings under the new commitment without feeling that they have lost a chance to change their mind. Engagements are a period of trial to test your relationship under "firm commitments" to each other. Many find that it was a lot of fun to date, but once they are committed they feel the other person is too demanding or domineering, and that they expect too much or don't give as much as they had expected. There are those who would like to break their engagements, but the social pressure is too great and they decide that they would rather go through with the marriage than face the embarrassment. This is very sad, because the engagement has not then fulfilled its purpose to be a testing period and a trial period. If the couple had been engaged secretly at first for a while, then they could both save each other this kind of embarrassment. It can also be helpful to avoid announcing any specific dates for a marriage. Everyone will want to know, but you can generalize with an answer that you haven't decided on any specific time as yet.

ENGAGEMENTS CAN CHANGE MANY THINGS!

So much of our dating is encased in the niceties of our best dress, our best manners and our best personality. During the engagement we should *make sure that we know what the person is really like to live with.* The fellow needs to see the girl in curlers and looking her worst. The girl needs to see the fellow under the car with grease on his hands and face. This might be accomplished by some surprise calls. We need to be with each other when things aren't working out the way we want them to. We should see each other when we are in the depths of dispair and discouragement. We need to see each other's temper at its worst. (If you are going to live with a temper and impatience for 40 or more years, you have a right to see what it is going to be like!) We need to see a person under great pressure of work or term papers and finals. Everyone has a breaking point, and we need to find out just where that is and whether we can live with it or not. Next, we need to know if our companion can handle the situation when we reach our breaking point, which hopefully comes at different times! It is questionable whether two individuals with the same level of emotional temperament will compliment each other and be good for each other.

FELLOWS' EXPECTATION OF AUTHORITY: It is an interesting paradox that takes place between dating and engagement. Often a fellow begins the relationship by bending over backwards to please the girl and provide for her every wish and request. He begs for the dates and pleads to make her happy in every way. He chases her until she catches him, and then the trend reverses in some levels. *Once engaged, the fellow expects much more from the girl.* He expects her to start pleasing him with her undivided attention. He expects her to be more submissive to his leadership role. As the fellow plays the dominant role that he believes he should as a man, many girls fear that their lover has turned into a rude and demanding brute who wants his own selfish way all the time. An engagement period is a time when both individuals start to understand the marriage expectations of the other and to assert a few of their own. It is truly a testing period to ascertain if they can weather the demands that married life will require.

KEEP YOUR EYES OPEN DURING THE ENGAGEMENT! The engagement period is a good period for more indepth discussions of how both of you feel about all phases of life, politics, religion, families, etc. Talk about their family and try to understand what kind of a concept they have of marriage and the roles of each partner. Many make the mistake of assuming that everyone sees marriage just as they do, but this is not so. You basically see the roles of "mother" and "dad" as you have observed them in your own home. You may have major plans to change certain things, but the basics will often remain from the example that was set for you. An engaged couple would be wise to spend as much time as possible around their partner's family. Observe how your partner treats all members of the family. And don't be so naive as to believe that they will be that much different when *you* are their new family. We should keep our eyes wide open during dating and engagement--but remember to keep them partly closed *after* marriage to the faults and failings of our partners!

HOW LONG OF AN ENGAGEMENT IS RECOMMENDED?

Obviously this depends on many factors. How long have you known each other? How long have you been going together? How long have you gone together in more serious dating, where you are considering marriage to each other? What kind of dating have you done? Has it been mostly by moon light or have you done meaningful things together? Have you gotten to know the person in a variety of situations? Have you really worked together on anything of consequence? Do you know how well you can work out problems together? Do you know the families of each other? Have other romances been put aside emotionally? How old are both of you? Do you have any economical way of supporting the marriage?

As you can see, each of these areas might suggest to different couples that they could use more time to good advantage, in getting to know each other even better. Wisdom might dictate that you should have a longer engagement. Next, let's cover some of the above areas in a little more detail.

Marriage before High School Graduation: If either of you are in high school, and especially the fellow, then you should postpone your marriage *until after graduation,* no matter how madly in love you are, or how sure you are that you are right for each other! Everything is against the success of your marriage. Employment opportunities, social acceptance, maturity reasons, etc. If you really love each other, you should love enough to put your marriage off so that you can increase the chances of having it succeed! If you are in high school then, your engagement should be long enough to at least include the graduation of both of you, if possible. And it would be even better to put the engagement off until after graduation. Values, interests and outlook on life change a great deal the first year after graduation, and success in marriage can be greatly increased by weathering these big changes. Some people will be offended by this writing, but all they need to do is look at some divorce rate statistics of those that marry during high school, and they will realize that they can double their chances of succeeding by waiting at least until after graduation! As far as the divorce rate is concerned, the older you get, the faster it goes down. But the speed in the decline is not as significant or important the first two years after high school graduation. The age is really not so significant after that either. The thing that becomes important after this period is how fast you rush into marriage without really knowing the person.

A Successful Engagement: Before we can have a successful marriage we ought to try to have a *SUCCESSFUL ENGAGEMENT!* A successful engagement will be one that is long enough to help you get to know the person in ways that you couldn't before you were thus committed to each other. You learn how devoted your partner is to you and how demanding you are to each other.

Length of Engagement: It appears from the author's research that most marriage counselors would recommend a *full year of engagement before marriage* to be safe. If you haven't known the person very long, the author would agree that a year would be advisable. Why so long? An individual can change drastically from one situation to another, from one environment to another. I have dated girls for a couple of years very heavily before finally discovering them to be very different individuals than I had thought them to be. It just takes a good long period of time to uncover many things and to carry on the process of blending your two personalities together.

But assuming that you have known each other during more than a year of very heavy dating, the author feels that a year of engagement isn't needed--provided that you have had a great deal of variety in your dating, that you have spent some long hours in each other's company, and that you have been involved in working with each other on some very worthwhile projects. Then in the author's judgement, the year could be shortened to six months and maybe even less, depending on how long you have known each other and how much of that time has been involved in problem-solving situations together.

The author always finds himself very disappointed when he hears of friends becoming engaged with plans of getting married several years away. It seems like if they are really that committed to each other, they ought to plan school and other things around their marriage instead of planning marriage around everything else. Yes, there will be hardships, but those kind of sacrifices make the marriage even more special and meaningful. If there is really love and desire for marriage, then it seems that they should be getting on with the marriage after they satisfy the safe guards of a reasonable engagement period.

"THOSE WHO CAN AFFORD IT"

The bride, white of hair, is stooped over her
cane,
Her footsteps, uncertain, need guiding.
While down the church aisle, with a wan tooth-
less smile,
The groom in a wheelchair comes riding.

And who are this elderly couple, thus wed?
You'll find when you've closely explored it,
That here is that rare, most conservative pair
Who waited until they could afford it.

Summary: In short, you are ready for marriage when you feel a real dependance upon your fellow or girl--when you feel spiritually, intellectually and emotionally committed, and when you can't stand the thoughts of being without your companion.

KEY 18: DETERMINE WHAT YOUR DEEPER EMOTIONAL NEEDS REALLY ARE!

SECTION II

FOR OLD MAIDS AND BACHELORS -AND- ESPECIALLY FOR THOSE WHO CRITICIZE THEM!

An ordinary day in the life of an "old bachelor" is to be approached by ten previous acquaintances and asked: "Are you married yet? Why not? What's wrong with you? You're too fussy! You shouldn't procrastinate so much! The girl you're going with now is just right for you, what are you waiting for? You're not perfect, so how can you expect someone else to be perfect? You bachelors are nothing but a bunch of playboys and pleasure lovers who are not willing to take on the real responsibilities of life. There must be something drastically wrong with you."

If you think the above illustration is exaggerated, all you need to do is to follow some bachelor around that is getting just a little bit older, and you will hear some of the above statements all the time. How does the bachelor respond to the questions? He covers up with standard comebacks: "No, I'm a confirmed bachelor. I don't want to lose my freedom." Then he gets a long lecture on his duty to society and the fact that he is keeping some poor girl single. Just how is an old bachelor supposed to respond? What is it you want to hear? Should he break down and cry on the spot? Is he to give you the intimate details of his many failures? Do you want him to plead for your sympathy for his latest broken romances? Would it help if he listed the number of marriage proposals he has made lately? Obviously he can't do any of these things, and so he covers up and acts as big, tough and as casual as he can and says "he's not interested in marriage."

If you knew the truth, you would soon find out that most bachelors are very anxious to find someone, and the fact that they haven't bothers them a great deal. In fact, many of them are extremely emotional about the whole topic once you know the truth. Yes, there are some who are procrastinating for one reason or another, and who are not doing much toward finding someone; but the vast majority are most anxious and would be willing to do nearly anything to find someone that they can feel happy with. Some are so deeply lonely and heartsick about being single, that they will often suffer long periods of depression. After so long they declare to themselves that they can't continue to live in depression and will structure their minds to *ignore* their longings for a companion and to try to enjoy being single. For sanity reasons they must adjust and do learn to enjoy life as a single person without too much depression.

Many bachelors are very involved with trying to convince some person to marry them, or they may just be getting over some disappointing relationship. But it isn't masculine to wear your heart on your sleeve--so they give some silly reply to get off the hook. The reason they are not married is really very ironically simple! They are not married for the same reason that someone younger than them isn't married. They have yet to find a person that they feel right about marrying, who is also interested in them. Now isn't that complicated? If some people could only realize how rude they are being in their pushy remarks to older singles! Their crudeness is only exceeded by their ignorance of the real situation.

When people have been married for a while they look back at the dating experience and remember mainly their successes. It seems to them that it was very easy to make the decision to get married; all there was to it was to simply make the decision. And maybe for a few people it was very simple, but most of them have forgotten what it was really like! Marrieds are in a totally different world than singles--they look at life differently, and think differently--they can't hope to understand fully what a single person is going through. And if they married relatively young they can never hope to comprehend what older bachelors and older maids are going through!

Age is a very relative situation. I have heard old bachelors criticize fellows older than themselves for not being married and ask the same ridiculous questions they are being asked: "Why aren't you married, what's your problem?" They are certain that they will never be as old as them when they get married! Why, they would do something drastic by then if they had to, they would just run out and marry the most likely thing around. But as they themselves arrive at that older age, they suddenly realize that the same prerequisite conditions are forever present. For they *MUST* feel *RIGHT* about it! The world seems to be full of intolerance and inability to understand other individuals in a different station and position in life than their own.

Many marrieds are very successful in conveying to the singles their total disgust for them. The singles can do nothing that will please them. Talk about a "generation gap," there is a larger "marital gap." They look upon the older singles as great oddities, as strange, as abnormals. If the singles don't date very often--they need to date more. If they date all the time, constantly, then they should date less. If they are dating many, they should stop and date just a few or one. If they are just dating one, then the experienced marrieds will say that they need to get out and date more people. It doesn't matter what they are doing or what their approach is, they are always doing it wrong!

LEADERS: The situation becomes even sadder when the leaders of single people, and especially their religious leaders, show great intolerance for them. It is fine when they teach the importance of marriage, it is fine when they encourage more dating, it is fine when they show a genuine interest in our progress; but they *violate their sacred trust as our leaders* when they begin to ridicule us, to make light-minded remarks about our situations, and when they start to "preach" to us all of the time about getting married. From our leaders we want understanding and encouragement, not insinuations and insults! The author has heard a few religious leaders mock their single followers when the singles inferred that they didn't have anyone that they felt right about marrying, and that they felt they must feel more right and certain about marriage before jumping into it. The leaders have responded with, "Well you don't need to hear voices from heaven or have an angel visit you in order to go ahead with a marriage." This is mockery to a person's faith--no single expects a heavenly manifestation, but they do rightfully expect to feel good about the decision! There must be some feeling of "rightness" about the whole thing! It bothers the author deeply to hear leaders make a "joke" of some person's single state!

The author was once asked to write a short article in a newsletter of a group he belonged to, and it went like this:

LIFE'S DECISIONS

> How are you keeping up with life's decisions? How are you holding up to the advances of supposed friends who would have you know that something is drastically wrong with you? Do you have a formula worked out in your mind as to how you will make your important decisions? When there are choices, do you plan to pull straws, give a count-down to 20, or spin a used apple core? Better yet, do you close your eyes and point to a blurred copy of a phone directory?
>
> Some fools would have you relegate certain life decisions to mere computer elimination and mechanical selection. If that isn't the answer, then what is? It is simply this! There is a God who loves you and me and who is concerned about our life's success and happiness and who has sacredly committed himself to the promise of helping us in our lives. How dare any crude person suggest that we should settle for anything less than a witness from our divine Maker? Or mock us further by saying that angels needn't tap us on the shoulder? Any person with any spiritual awareness knows when he is *at*

peace within himself. That is all we seek and rightfully deserve. If we make decisions upon any other grounds, do we really need the truths of religion? I personally pity the individual who submits himself to outward pressures and enticements in making any of life's really important decisions. It has nothing to do with how wonderful the choices are, but--can you feel *at one* with yourself? To this reality may we all hold fast! *J.D.H.*

To everything there is a season, and a time....A time to be born, a time to die. A time to weep, and a time to laugh; a time to mourn, and a time to dance. A time to love, and a time to hate; a time of war, and a time of peace. (Ecclesiastes 3)

GIRLS' POSITION: The comments of this chapter apply to the girls as well as the fellows. There are endless unkind remarks made against the girls who are still single. In many people's way of thinking it is considered a much worse plight to be an "old maid," than it is to be an "old bachelor." However, the "old maids" are usually looked upon with a "quiet pity," while their counter parts, "old bachelors," are looked upon with total disgust. The poor old gal can't help herself, it is all the fault of that lazy good-for-nothing bachelor who is keeping her single. Yes, the girls are somewhat at the mercy of the fellows; but it is a two-way street! Some of the most homely-looking girls I have ever seen are dating all the time, because they are out-going and friendly. They know how to make a fellow feel welcome and how to encourage him all the way through the dating relationship. They are married long before some of their friends who are often the most beautiful shapely creatures you can imagine--but who turn fellows down left and right and never allow a fellow to develop a meaningful relationship with them. The girl often waits for the fellow to do the asking, but once the girl has been asked, then it is the fellow who is entirely at the "mercy" of the girl! And as he does everything he can to promote the relationship, he again is entirely at the "mercy" of the girl. The responsibility of relationships failing must be justly shared with both the girl and the fellow. They both have the opportunity to promote or to discourage any given situation! If a girl doesn't feel that she wants to accept dates with a fellow, she shouldn't accept them! If she doesn't want to marry a fellow, she shouldn't marry him! But likewise a fellow has the same moral obligation to himself to drop anyone and everyone that he doesn't feel right about.

THERE'S NOTHING TO JUST GETTING MARRIED: When the marrieds tell the singles that it is about time they get married, they often make it sound so easy, just like if you were going downtown to buy an overcoat. When it comes right down to it, it really wouldn't be very difficult to "just" get married. Even the saddest looking girls and the most unhandsome fellows wouldn't have any difficulty finding "something" to marry if that were all they were trying to achieve. If they would forget all about their basic requirements of a congenial personality, honesty and trustworthiness, some degree of intelligence; if they would forget about liking or wanting the person, not to mention love, then it would be a snap! Nothing to it! Anyone that has done any dating knows that there is always someone that "likes" you. You usually don't have any interest in them and hardly know that they exist, or else you are strongly repulsed by them! Now, if *everyone* would just forget about not liking or wanting someone else, then all the singles in the world could be married overnight! There's nothing to just getting married.

But some foolish married people have really forgotten what it's like. They have forgotten that simple and basic emotional experience--*TO WANT SOMEBODY!* The joy of getting married would be hollow, meaningless and void without *WANTING* the person you are marrying. And the whole paradox of the dating world is that you can never seem to find a situation where you both want each other strongly enough to get married. It always seems that those you want badly can't see anything in you, and vice versa.

"What is your problem? Why aren't you married?" The answer should be plain by now. Again, the inference is that single people have a lot of unusual problems and that they are abnormal. If you will get out and mix with old bachelors and old maids you will find that they are more often than not, a very highly educated, skilled and intelligent group of people! And the only basic difference between them and married people is that the marrieds have found someone with whom there is a mutual "wanting and desire."

In summary, then, it doesn't matter how old you are or how long you have dated some person, or how much they have done for you. It doesn't matter how many others think it is right, you're the one that has to live with that person, and not them. It has nothing to do with how outstanding the person is, or what a prize catch they would be for you. It doesn't matter how rich they are, or what experiences they have behind them, or how smart they are. You can have endless experience with them and appreciate them in a most deep and meaningful way. You may even feel a deep human love for them; but you may still lack the desire to marry them. You may love a person for all they have done for you, but it may not be a marital-type love. Married people often forget that the reason they are happy in their marriage is that they have someone they *EMOTIONALLY WANT, and they should allow everyone else the same privilege.*

When should you get married? *When you feel right about it, and when you both want each other and not a moment sooner!* As one wise religious leader put it: "Never marry unless the Spirit of God bears witness that you are getting a companion for all eternity as well as for time. It is better not to marry at all, than to do so contrary to this principle." (J.F.S.)

Chapter 5

WHAT IS LOVE?

SECTION I—LOVE DEFINED

The whole world wants love, everyone seeks love and we all are dying for more love, but who can even define it? Many claim it is an abstract and is non-definable. The author has had the experience of getting several groups together to discuss what love is. It has been a fun evening sometimes, but often the differing opinions are presented with so much zeal that any love present in the group has all but disappeared. The participants have had different experiences and have concluded that "Love" is what they have experienced. Many have been overly influenced by Hollywood romances on one extreme, and by "old married experts" who have been married far too long to remember what love is like before marriage on the other extreme. Most of the differences turn out to be only semantic--just differences in the way words are used. It doesn't matter what we call various kinds of love so long as we understand each other. Words are merely symbols that we use to represent concepts. If someone wishes to call a certain kind of love "blue," then that's fine, just so we understand what they are describing. Following this line of reasoning, permit the writer to develop a pattern of symbols which will be useful in describing and understanding the illusive emotion we label as "Love."

It is fun to write poetry and create endless descriptions of love. The author has personally gathered many hundreds of definitions directly from individuals and from writings. These are beautiful descriptions of what people felt in particular romances at specific periods of the romance. But these kinds of definitions are of little help to someone that doesn't know what love is and who is attempting to discover if they have arrived at the pinnacle of emotional feeling we call love. We are often guilty of defining love with too many adjectives, and we create an illusive enigma, something that is so totally incomprehensible and non-existent. Daters of all ages are mislead into believing that love is always something else than what they have yet experienced. There is an urgent need to define love as simply as we can, to provide a definition that will be more inclusive of everyone's experience with love, and to exclude the perplexities of exotic definitions. The author suggests the following definition be used for purposes of proceeding with our study on the subject of love. There will be further discussion to explain why this select grouping of words was used.

LOVE IS: "A PERSISTENT EMOTIONAL YEARNING TO BE WITH SOMEONE!!!"

HOW MANY ABSOLUTES ARE THERE IN LOVE?

After endless hours of listening to individuals attempt to define love, and observing people struggle with trying to experience love, the author has made an interesting discovery. Those individuals who have the greatest problems with defining or experiencing love always attempt to make love far too ABSOLUTE! It is all or nothing. They often make some of the following statements about love:

1. Love is something you only experience in marriage or just prior to marriage.
2. Love cannot be experienced early in a relationship, it has to develop over a long period of time.
3. Love is something that you only experience with one person.

4. If your courtship doesn't work out, or even if your marriage fails, then it wasn't true love.

These kinds of statements are greatly lacking in depth and truth. People who make these kinds of statements are probably sincere, but they mistakenly believe everyone else will experience love as they did. They often make these mistakes for the following three reasons:

1st: They lack the variety of experiences in their dating or they may have dated very few!
2nd: They may have had the experiences, but they have forgotten what it was really like.
3rd: They may even remember what it was like, but they have never really stopped to analyze the possibilities with any real depth of consideration.

Whatever their reasons were for defining love in these absolute terms, the result is nonetheless very harmful. Those who listen to learn from them pursue their quest for love, with the understanding that they will not have arrived until those absolute conditions are fulfilled. And along with these basic absolutes they add many other little foolish notions of things they have heard someone say about their particular experience with love. And so the foolishness is perpetuated and people are made unhappy because they are so unlucky to never arrive at the glorious stage of love as they have been given to understand it. And no matter how beautiful their relationship might be with a person, they would never think of becoming married to that individual simply because love is not present, as they understand love. And no one can marry without love!? Can you perceive how great the tragedy can be for daters to espouse false convictions of what love is really all about?

In conclusion, the author would send forth his plea again for those who wish to define love, to at least begin with a definition that explains love in all its simplicity. Why not begin with: *Love is: A persistent emotional yearning to be with someone.*

THE CONFUSION OF MISS X IN RECOGNIZING LOVE

Illustrations usually help explain things, and the issues just covered are so critical that the author will select just one real life situation from one of so many the author has either experienced or observed at close range.

Miss X: A certain young man dated hundreds of girls, and felt he had experienced some real genuine love for several of them during his college years. Then came graduation with a Master's Degree, and he was sent out into the world to continue his search for that "special" girl away from college. He was lined up on a blind date with a girl who became nearly a constant companion for about three years. She seemed to have every single talent and skill that he had ever dreamed of having in one person. It seemed that all five areas of love were there in great abundance. (The five areas will be introduced soon.)

The romance involved a series of exciting projects, and the girl was out of work at the time, so she worked full time on these projects for many long months. Long hours every day with the fellow produced ample experience to proceed into the commitment stages of the courtship. But as usual, she was still not able to verbally admit that she had experienced any feeling of love. She finally obtained another job and began working. During her brief lunch break it was very common for her to travel many miles to just be with her boyfriend for just a few minutes of that time. She involved herself in endless ways to make the relationship extra special. There were all the outward signs of love eminating from her being. But when it came right down to the point of talking about the word "love," she was never quite able to verbalize any commitment.

She was hung up on the concept that love was something she probably hadn't experienced yet in her life and most likely wouldn't until she was near the altar, and only then if it were really the right thing. She wasn't completely sure what she was supposed to feel, but her concept of love (or her lack of concept) was constantly in the way of the relationship being able to progress. She often had that confused and hurt look from struggling with her fairy tale stage of love she had been taught by someone, or had self-imposed into her imagination. Even though she had some feelings and was often extremely excited with the relationship, she could never uncover the word "love," as if to do so would be immoral. The couple analyzed it and analyzed it until there was paralysis of analysis. Hardening of the love arteries set in and the relationship died.

Some might propose that there just wasn't sufficient love to proceed to marriage, and that may have been, but the singular problem was still one of understanding and accepting the obvious elements and emotions of love that were so definitely present. The author has seen countless other old maids and bachelors with this same hang-up of not understanding what the mysterious thing called love was supposed to involve, and wondering if they were in love or not. In so many cases, a simple and concise definition of love could have been a great help to them.

People have trouble with love in and out of marriage because of the unreasonable demands they put on what they think is "love." They expect far too much out of love, and therefore their experience with it is always a disappointment to them. They never seem fulfilled enough with love. Therefore they make their own lives and the lives of their partners miserable and unhappy.

HOW LONG BEFORE LOVE CAN STRIKE?

The story is told of a great religious leader who complimented his wife by telling her on one of their anniversaries late in life: "I thought I loved you when I married you, but when I compare my love for you now, I'm not sure I did." This beautiful illustration is often misused to belittle the great feelings of love that young people have for each other. I have heard it used to teach that love can only be developed over the years and that it doesn't even exist before marriage, when it should only be used to illustrate that love can continue to grow infinitely more beautiful over the years if properly cared for. Love does exist in younger years, and it can be just as dynamically all-consuming to an individual in his present sphere of existence as in his future.

SLOW DEVELOPING LOVE: Many courtships don't experience a great deal of love to begin with, but over many long months and sometimes even years, they can develop into a relationship of great love. The author has had several such relationships. One in particular was interesting, because he was really quite repulsed by the girl around the second date--not so much because of her, but because of the contrast in personality to a girl he was madly in love with at the time. He had no further intentions of dating her, but she continued to promote the relationship by inviting him to dinners and special dances and being conveniently around at times. This casual friendship lasted several years before the writer realized that it had quietly grown to be one of the most significant relationships in his life. So many relationships which develop slowly do turn out to be very significant. But as young daters we don't usually want it to happen this way, we are too impatient and want it to start off with a bang. And besides, it doesn't sound to us like the usual Hollywood-type romance if there isn't a great dose of love to begin with.

FAST DEVELOPING LOVE: As the author can bear witness that love does often develop slowly, he wants to be quick in asserting that it can also be experienced quickly. So many old fogies insist that it must take time to develop simply because that is the way it happened to them. And yet there are so many who have had the opposite experience, of love being felt immediately. The author knows what it is like to feel strong, deep emotional yearnings for a person, and to have these feelings persist so dominantly that he has found it difficult to think about or accomplish little else. He knows what the feelings were like, and he is also able to declare solemnly that he has felt those same urgent emotions on many first dates and second dates! He knows extremely well a young lady who stated that she had felt so much of the emotions of love on the first date, as did her companion, that they began talking about marriage on that *first date.* They were happily married a number of months later. And this has happened to other couples of the author's acquaintance, who knew upon first meeting their partner that he or she was the one they were to marry. Those kinds of feelings are more than mere attraction--it takes love.

Nearly everyone who dates a great deal has experienced occasionally those early floods of emotion and love. Far too often they are one-sided and the relationships fail, but that in no way diminishes the reality and validity of those feelings of love.

LOVE KNOWS NO STRUCTURED LIST OF CONDITIONS: Love has no structured timetable, it knows no clock. It requires no list of logical items we must first know about the person. It relies only upon our feelings. We don't have to be married many years, nor just about ready to be married, nor do we have to turn a certain magical age to suddenly become qualified to experience that oldest of emotions, that old fashioned thing called love. We don't have to have a specified number of dates before we experience it, nor does a superficial date on the calendar suddenly qualify us to begin experiencing a loving yearning for another person. It doesn't matter whether we know everything about the person or very little. It doesn't always distinguish between what is best or better for us. We may feel the emotions of love for the village tramp or we may be lucky enough to love the State's queen. We may love alone or we may share love. WE LOVE IN FOOLISHNESS AND WE LOVE IN WISDOM, BUT THE EMOTIONS OF LOVE ARE MUCH THE SAME!

SECTION II

VARIATIONS OF LOVE

We have considered how love can be felt early in the relationship or can be developed over a period of time. At this point in the writing it would be useful to have some labels for the different stages we experience in love. The emotions may not really be that different, but the background is. They could be broken up in many ways, but the author has selected four.

PROGRESSIVE STAGES OF LOVE:

1. *Infatuated Love:*
   We know very little about the person. We may have never dated the person or we may have dated them very little. However, we are very emotionally excited about sharing their companionship as much as possible. The emotional yearnings may be foolish and may end any time, but for now they are continual and persistent. Many may say our feelings are not "real love" and call them mere infatuation, but as far as we are concerned, our love is very much a reality.
2. *Experienced Love:*
   We know the person very well, we know their strengths and weaknesses, we have dated the person long enough to know how we affect each other socially and psychologically. We have a clear awareness of how we fulfill each other's needs. And even through this intellectual knowledge and experience we still have a strong emotional desire which is persistent in creating a yearning for us to be with them.
3. *Committed Love:*
   Hopefully we have the background of "experienced love," but it isn't always the case. We have progressed to the point that we are very much concerned for the future welfare and happiness of our companion. Of our own volition we have already stopped dating others and are giving our companion our full attention, or we are at least willing to do so if agreed upon between us. Our commitments may be just verbal or they may be through some token, like a pin. Eventually we are willing to progress to full engagement. We are anxious to show love through actions of devotion.

4. *Marital Love:*
   The love we experience in marriage will depend upon the couple, but to endure, it must include a total commitment of devotion to ignore all other emotional impulses of love we may feel for others. Hopefully, we are as committed to our companion's happiness as we are to our own. Sometimes the emotional drive and urgency of love is less dominant and all-consuming than in earlier stages of love, simply because we are not persistently striving to win them and possess them as before marriage. It is common for the actions of love to be more present than the emotions. The emotions of love are taken a little more for granted and there is often a peaceful assurance that we have married the best person for us.

A person's progress between these various stages of love is not always distinguishable, but hopefully for our sake, there is progress being made, and we are continuing to feel a persistent emotional yearning to be with our companion.

We have talked about the various stages of love through which we can progress, but this doesn't cover the different areas in which we can love a person. The basic emotion of love is the same, but it can take on a large variety of meanings. Different people fulfill us in different ways. We will never experience love quite the same way twice even if it were possible to find an identical twin in looks and personality, simply because we are always changing in our own personality due to our experiences and chances for learning. Furthermore, the sequence of events that produced a former romance will never be identical either. There are literally thousands upon thousands of variables to every romance. However, it is not difficult to group some of these variable areas, and the author has selected the five following areas:

FIVE AREAS OF LOVE:

1. *Physical Love:*
   We feel the person is beautiful or handsome. We are excited to look into their eyes, hold their hand, put our

arms around them and enjoy the thought of kissing them. We have a persistent emotional yearning to want to be close to their being.

2. *Friendship Love:*
   We have discovered someone that we are anxious to be a genuine friend to. We are concerned for their welfare and happiness. We support them in all their goals and aspirations and wish to be a motivating force to encourage them in life. We have a constant yearning to be of help and service to them and to demonstrate our friendship.
3. *Social Love:*
   We are excited about their personality and want to be around them as much as is reasonably possible. We feel like we have more fun with them than anyone. We enjoy certain kinds of social activity with them. Maybe it is dancing, socializing with a group, some sporting activity, etc. Often we enjoy their sense of humour. Their personality blends beautifully with ours, and we miss them greatly when we are away from them.
4. *Intellectual Love:*
   We may be emotionally involved with an admiration for their intelligence. It either blends with ours or is superior. We yearn to visit with them and talk about many things. We feel we can communicate with each other and understand each other's point of view. We don't necessarily agree on everything, but we share common points of view on most things. We feel stimulated by their mind.
5. *Spiritual Love:*
   We share common moral beliefs and goals. This often includes the same thoughts about God, and we often share the same religious convictions. We are spiritual equals, or we feel extremely impressed with their spirituality or their strong moral convictions. We share the same moral beliefs about honesty, virtue and ideals about serving our fellow men. Our dates often involve religious or service experiences. We are emotionally anxious to be with them and experience a spiritual love and unity.

EMOTIONAL DEPENDANCE FOR CERTAIN AREAS OF LOVE

The author has observed in his dating experience that after he has dated a girl with outstanding qualities in one of these areas, he often feels a great lack in this area with other girls--especially when he has dated the person for a long time and has developed some *emotional dependance* for those particular kinds of attributes. Sometimes you are outwardly comparing and looking for the same things in someone else, sometimes you may concentrate on not comparing, but subconsciously and emotionally you cannot deny the need you feel for those certain attributes.

To illustrate what the author is talking about, let's create the following example: Let's say you date a person for a good while that is very intellectually stimulating to you. In other words, you discover you feel some intellectual love for them. They have a quick wit and they are able to understand your every thought. You have a persistent emotional yearning to be with them. You enjoy the great stimulation you get from just sitting and visiting with them.

After a period of time however, you decide that their looks are not as exciting as you feel they must be in order to marry them. So you find some movie star-looking individual that stirs every physical fiber of your being. You are physically in love with them from the start. But then as you attempt to develop the relationship with them, you find they are shallow, without any real depth intellectually; they don't understand so many things that you say to them. You stay with it for a few months longer and finally discover that they are socially very mature and that they are just a lot of fun to be with; and so you become encouraged and develop a spark of social love for them that makes you want to be with them every minute you can.

After some more time passes and you try to develop the commitment stages of your romance, you discover that you are still greatly bothered about their lack of intellectual depth and feel all of a sudden you have made a big mistake. It is really the other person that you love most. So you go back to them and try to make the relationship work, but by way of recent comparison, you suddenly discover how ugly they really are, and suddenly you realize that the person has no social graces. They seem awkward and clumsy in so many ways that you had never noticed before. What do you do now, run back to the other person? Or do you go out and seek another person that may lack the attributes of both of these individuals?

Is the above example farfetched? Not at all. Those who do very much dating experience it all the time. The author is convinced that it is one of the main reasons why older singles find it even more difficult to be real happy with any one person. They have had some deep romances with individuals who were outstanding in certain areas, they felt a great "love" for the individual in those areas, and they are forever more having a "longing" to find that same fulfillment in some other person, and especially the person of their dreams.

To be able to intellectually realize the above phenomenon ought to be a great help in more successful dating. Because once we accept the fact that it is happening to us, hopefully we can take steps to minimize the effects it may have upon our dating and in trying to develop new relationships.

COMPOSITE NEEDED: It is obvious that we need a composite of all these areas. We must be somewhat fulfilled in all of the areas to some degree. On the other hand, we must accept the fact that everyone is stronger in some areas than others, and we will never find anyone that is more outstanding than every other human being in all the areas. Therefore we must select those areas that are most important to us and find someone who fulfills us in those areas and who is also at least acceptable in some of the other areas. Easier said than done, but herein lies one of the great secrets to successful dating!

WISE LOVE VERSUS FOOLISH LOVE

So often we assume that because it is love, it is right, it is good, it is wise. Or we say that it isn't love unless it is wise. It is hoped that we have already illustrated that the latter is not true, that the emotions of love knows no logic or conditions.

As a result, we have young people often throwing their lives away by simply allowing the emotions of love to dictate their actions of immorality and of marrying those who would not be good for them.

Everyone knows examples of friends and acquaintances who have made some foolish decisions in marriage which were obvious to everyone else but them. And no effort, persuasion, counseling or reasoning would dissuade them from taking the steps. They would often forsake their religion, their families, their educational training and their culture to be true to their foolish emotions of love. How many have known of sweet young ladies who were as devout to their religion as they could be, only to dissolve all connections simply because that is the way their husbands wanted it to be. It matters not if they are atheist, agnostic or a hater of some religious faith.

I remember one wise Doctor speaking to a group of young people many years ago and stating that "A woman in love is at her lowest point of intelligence." I have thought about that over the years and have observed that it is all too often true. I'm not so sure that it just applies to the women; but probably more so, because they are more the submitting vessels to be accomodating to their lovers' wishes. Others have called love "blind," for there is certainly a blinding effect. We are unable to see weakness and failings. Being aware of these things should help us to use the extra caution we need with those we accept any dates with and those who we continue to date. And even if we should find ourselves in love, we should cut the relationship off if we know that they aren't good for us. You can still admit love, without loving unto marriage.

The author will list four areas of foolish love:

1. *Selfish Love:* There are those who are basically selfish and have never learned to be giving. Their emotions of love may be as sincere as they know how to be. But they will love you for what they can get out of you only. Maybe you're wealthy, maybe you are famous, or maybe they can just get you to do a lot of things for them without doing anything in return. They are often guilty of being concerned only for their own happiness, and they just don't have your best interest at heart.

2. *Immoral Love:* Some love for physical reasons only. The emotions of love may be there in full bloom, but only in their specialized context. An immoral love is a selfish love, for they love you for only what they can get out of you sexually. Some mistakenly think you must prove your love sexually, which is the most insidious type of lie that you can make, for a mature and healthy love wishes only the best for their partner and is concerned with their happiness--which is totally absent in this kind of love. Sexual desire is present in and out of love and has nothing to do with proving love--it disproves it if anything.

3. *Qualified Love:* This is the type of love that seems to keep terminating if you don't keep qualifying with the specified conditions. It is also a type of selfish love and an immature love. The emotions of love and romance are there as long as the fellow takes the girl to expensive places and showers her with gifts. He loves her only if she types his papers, and does his bidding. It is often difficult to distinguish between disappointment from unfulfilled expectations and a genuine decrease in love, because expectation levels are so deeply intertwined with the building blocks of love. Also, we are all different in how demanding we are as a personality. A demanding person will always appear to demonstrate qualifications for his love. As complicated as it can be, it is still an intelligent idea to keep an eye open for those who seem to demand an unusual amount of demonstration for giving their love to you, and love based upon too many qualifications. Do they love you, or do they just love a few of the things you can do for them?

4. *Immature Love:* This is the kind of love that ignores all of the unhealthy conditions of both your loves. Maybe you quarrel and argue all of the time. The immature lover has to always have it his way, no give and take. Your backgrounds are too drastically different, too varied in age, religion, culture, or education for a happy marriage to result; but in an immature love, you ignore these obvious signs and push toward marriage anyway. You are too young to make commitments but you do anyway. You defy the wisdom of parents, counselors, and friends. You ignore what is best or better and seek only to gratify the emotional response you feel. You may not be happy

with each other and you know the relationship is no good, but you refuse to break up because the emotions of love have tied you together.

MATURE LOVE: It has very little to do with the intensity of the love, but more with the qualities of the love. You are more concerned with the happiness of your partner than they are with their own. You are both willing to accept the responsibilities of the love, give and take. You listen to the counsel of others and are willing to do what is best, to wait, to date others, and even break up in the best interest of the other.

FRIENDSHIP VERSUS LOVE

In the famous movie, "Shenandoah," James Stewart was approached by a young man who was crazy about his daughter and who wanted to marry her. He asked why the boy wanted to marry her. The boy replied that he was madly in love with her. James Stewart replied: "That's obvious, but do you like her?"

DO YOU LIKE HER? This is a great question to ask ourselves as we jump into the commitment stages of love. It is usually presumed that first you like someone and then you love them. But it isn't necessarily always true--our emotions can carry us away into a frantic state of love and romance before we have really developed a sound friendship. There are times when a young couple jumps right into areas of physical love, kissing and making love without really knowing that much about each other's backgrounds. Sometimes they haven't really discovered even the other's personality, their goals, aspirations and what they really want out of life. They may know very little about what it is like to work and live with the other person. All they know is that every time they have been together they have had a great time making love, and so they call it "love." The author would not question for a moment that they are in love, very likely they have a persistent emotional yearning to be with each other. They may think of nothing else when they are separated, but being with each other again. It matters little if they have had twenty-five dates or one, they are sold on each other and are feeling the genuine emotions of love in the specific area of "physical love."

WELL-BALANCED LOVE: It is really quite common for many relationships to develop too rapidly into the areas of physical love, without having a firm basis of learning to like the person in friendship. To those around them they are involved in a "foolish love." Intelligence would decree that it will remain a foolish love until they drop back and develop a love for each other in several of the other areas of love, and especially in the basic area of friendship. After marriage the areas of friendship and intellectual compatibility have a lot more to do with keeping a relationship together and happy. Unhappy marriages can often be traced back to situations where the couple did not develop some degree of love for each other in most or all of the areas of love.

CAN YOU LOVE MORE THAN ONE PERSON AT A TIME?

Definitely you can! You love them for different reasons. Those who do a lot of dating often experience the conflict of feeling great emotions for more than one person and have difficulty in making decisions as a result. It is most common while you are breaking up with one person and starting to go with someone else. Dr. Richard Udr made a study at the University of North Carolina in which 25 percent of the girls claimed to be in love with two or more men at the same time. The study makes you wonder how many of the other 75 percent even claimed to love or even may have loved two men at other times. Knowing these things might make the 25 percent figure even more significant. The author even had one girl come back with an engagement ring on, but hidden in her pocket, to visit him and search her feelings once again before proceeding with the final arrangements of her marriage. It wasn't that she didn't love her future husband, but she also felt some strong feelings of love for the writer and was confused because of it.

In our system of monogamy we blindly get hooked up with the idea that it is an impossibility to love two individuals at the same time. In other parts of the world where polygamy is still common, they realize without doubt that human feelings are capable of having the emotions of love for more than one. The non-acceptance of the idea in our society creates unhappy marriages and is a contributing factor to some divorces. A man or woman discovers someone else that they have the capability of feeling some deep emotional yearnings for and because of the freshness of these emotions they are more intense than those feelings they have for their present companion. And so they blindly declare that they *no longer love* their present companions and seek a divorce. Or they are even more stupid and declare that they thought they had loved their companions, but they guess it *wasn't "real love,"* because they feel love for someone else.

This is one of the reasons that marriage is so special. You do possess the ability to love others, but you ignore these emotions when and if they come, and you refuse to allow them to develop or linger and reserve yourself for the one to whom you have made a sacred contract of devotion! *Love in marriage becomes more than an emotion, it becomes an action of devotion.*

QUESTIONNAIRE TO DETERMINE IF YOU ARE IN LOVE

As earlier stated, the author objects to lists that make love a certain composite of just certain things, so please do not accept this list as a rigid summary of all things. It may be that you are in love and don't answer these questions in the typical pattern. It is only given to help some determine their status based again on our earlier definition of: LOVE IS A PERSISTENT EMOTIONAL YEARNING TO BE WITH SOMEONE!

YES-NO

1. Do you find yourself thinking about the person a great deal of the time?
2. Are you always sorry when the date has to come to an end?
3. Do you find yourself persistently yearning to call them or be with them?
4. Would you rather be with them than anyone else?
5. Would you stop going with others if they asked you to?
6. Are you proud to be seen with the person and anxious for your closest friends to meet them?
7. Can you visualize spending the rest of your life with them?
8. Are you more concerned with their comfort and happiness than your own?
9. Are there at least three of the areas that you feel you are strongly in love with the person: (Physical, Friendship, Social, Intellectual, Spiritual)?
10. If marriage were possible in the near future, would you be all for it?

If you could answer any of these with a positive answer of yes, then chances are you are feeling some of the emotions of love, and the more you answered positively, the more assuredly you must be in love.

SECTION III

CREATING LOVE

Too many people see the problem of love as being loved more than loving--of finding the right person rather than being the right person. We need to spend more time learning to love instead of always being hung up on finding someone to love. As Eric Fromm puts it: *"Loving is an art that can be learned."*

HOW DOES ONE CREATE LOVE? With the wealth of ideas we have covered thus far, we should have some real helpful background and insights into ways to help ourselves in creating more love. Hopefully we now have a better concept of what love involves and understand love with a better set of definitions. We have a basic definition, we understand the four stages of love, the five areas of love, the difference between loving foolishly and loving wisely and we know something of how it often happens. Utilization of these concepts should help in creating more love.

However, there are some other topical areas that might be helpful in creating love. We have talked about the kinds of love, but we have yet to cover some of the basic components that make up love.

WHAT IS LOVE MADE UP OF? To begin with, love is made up of our THOUGHTS. Those thoughts that find their way to our heart usually come out as LOVE!

The thoughts are produced from our observations and experiences. We observe the things that are inviting to us and we experience things that are pleasant to us. Because we enjoy them our mind dwells on them persistently and enlarges upon them. Like thoughts gather similar and like thoughts, and our feelings grow and are intensified. The following is a suggested list of some of the elements that make up love:

ELEMENTS OF LOVE:

1. *Happy Thoughts* and pleasant experiences of our companions.
2. *Appreciation* for their kindness and considerations.
3. *Desire* to be with them and share their company.
4. *Anxiousness* to be kind, helpful and giving to them.
5. *Relaxed* and comfortable feeling around them.
6. *Romantic Atmosphere* that makes us feel close to them.
7. *Tenderness* for the feelings of the other.
8. *Concern* for their happiness and well-being.
9. *Protective Urge* to keep them from harm.
10. *Admiration* for the skills, talents and persons they are.
11. *Friendship* based on meaningful experience.

12. *Intrigue* and wonderment of how they feel about us and what the future holds.
13. *Imagination* to create fun times and to enlarge upon these times in the mind.
14. *Respect* for their character, ideals, and courage.
15. *Persistent Emotional Yearning* to be with them.

Now with a realization of some of the elements that make up love, we should be able to work with them.

ATMOSPHERE: Take the atmosphere, for example. We can attempt to take our girl to romantic places and do romantic things, and the girl can try to do her part by enjoying herself and acting interested and by inviting the fellow in to eat something at the end of the date. Remember, we are more prone to feel the stronger emotions of love by a lake side with a full moon. We are more prone to feel romantic when our favorite date is dressed up fit to kill.

CONCENTRATION: We are more prone to feel romantic when our minds are cleared from our problems of school or work or the home. We need to clear our minds and give our dates our full attention and show a genuine interest in them.

SPONTANEITY: We are more attracted to someone when they are natural and relaxed, and not so rigid, formal, business-like, reserved and structured. We enjoy being with someone that can let their hair down a little, enjoy a little humour and create fun out of just being in their company.

ADMIRATION: Realizing that admiration and respect are vital to love, we both can pay meaningful compliments to each other and make mention of those areas in which we admire and respect them. Let them know that they looked nice tonight, that it was a great idea to do this or that, that they performed well in their speech, music, sport, or whatever we saw them doing.

ADMIRATION AND MEN: Someone has said that men would rather be admired than loved, while women seek love and to know they are attractive. Whether it is totally true or not, there is a very dominant need in a man to be admired by his girl. And admiration is a form of love. He seeks approval for his actions and pictures himself being her hero in endless ways. Even when he is away from someone that he loves, he imagines them watching him, approving, and cheering him on. Women would be foolish not to use this knowledge to their advantage and be careful of ridiculing their men folk. And we know that a woman cannot love a man she feels to be her inferior; love without veneration and enthusiasm is only friendship.

The man, on the other hand, should remember that a woman wants to feel as feminine as he wants to feel masculine, and he should treat her like a lady so as to make her feel like one. Men need to be forever observant of women's special efforts to have their hair done, or to wear new items of clothing, etc.

Both men and women can show kindness and consideration in endless ways. It is alright to joke and tease, but be extra careful not to say those things that might offend and void the area of tenderness for their feelings.

INTRIGUE: Being aware that romance thrives on wonderment and intrigue, it would be foolish to take all that intrigue away by telling them all of our feelings for them too early. We can give them encouragement by letting them know of our interest, but say most of it with actions and interest and less with words. Romantic words and expressions can be present but shouldn't involve a full confession of our emotional commitment to them.

LOVE IS STRONGEST IN PURSUIT! We are always wanting someone that doesn't want us, and there is always someone wanting us that we don't want anything to do with. And a lot of it has to do with the fact that we create the emotions of love while in pursuit. As we pursue, we become more anxious, more desirous; and the more time and emotion we invest, the more urgent and intensified our emotions of love become.

LOVE & IMAGINATION: Love and romance are the results of a stimulated imagination! If we are attempting to develop the ability to love others more, we should keep in mind that love thrives on our ability to imagine. The imagination often blinds us to their weaknesses and magnifies their strengths all out of proportion. Our imagination sees their beauty and covers or screens their flaws. All great inventions are first imagined in the mind, and so it is with great actions of love. We first imagine ourselves going out with them--and it is accomplished. We imagine doing fun things with them--and it is accomplished. We imagine what it would be like to kiss them--and it is accomplished. We imagine what it would be like to go steady with them, to become engaged--and it may be accomplished. We imagine what it would be like to be married to them--and it might well be the very thing that is finally accomplished.

If we find someone that we know is good for us, and we would like to develop more feelings for them, we need to think of the areas in which we could most easily develop a feeling of love for them, and then concentrate on these areas. We can imagine pleasant things about them, think positively, and if there is any "rightness" to it, the relationship should develop. But if nothing comes of our positive affirmations, then it must not be any good for us, because *love must begin with a certain amount of natural desire!* If the whole idea becomes too repulsive, then our imagination has told us it isn't possible and we'd better drop them and look elsewhere. But remember: *Romance is the stimulation of the imagination.*

STEPS IN CREATING LOVE FOR SOMEONE

In summary of some of the things we have presented, we will suggest the following four steps that occur often while love is in the process of creation:

1st: *Some Natural Desire:*
We must begin with some interest or some spontaneous desire to be in their company. We may not have any emotional feeling for them, but if we welcome the idea of trying to develop an interest we are on our way.

2nd: *Patience:*
Knowing that all romances don't come immediately, we can show hope through our patience. We can continue to

date the person and try to learn as much about them as possible through varied experiences with them.

3rd: *Five Areas of Love:*

We can concentrate on looking for those attributes that we admire and respect. We can be more positive in our judgement of them and less critical. We know at least five basic areas in which we can feel love, so we can analyze which of these areas we are most likely to respect, admire and eventually feel love for. Then we can concentrate on these areas, observing and appreciating them for these strong points.

4th: *Use of Imagination:*

We know that a large part of the emotions of love stem from our imagination and memory. We can imagine ourselves with them in various situations and give some thought as to what we can do to make it more fun ana possibly romantic. We can allow our minds to dwell on the things that we like most about them. *We can't force love, but we can encourage it!* If there is any hope there, our thoughts will gather more like and similar thoughts, and we may soon develop some positive emotional response toward them that may grow into an emotional yearning to be with them. We may only love them in certain areas, but that is a start and we can eventually come to love a person in many areas.

It is always easier said than done, but who knows, it may be worth a try? If it doesn't work, we can always move on to greener pastures. We all dream of finding someone with whom all the pieces just fit together and there is a natural magnetic attraction for both individuals immediately. Some do experience this, but in the large majority of cases, at least one of the individuals has to develop these emotions of love over a long period of time. The older one gets, the more often this is the case. Remember that in the Victorian Age, one married and then looked for love; now in the modern Western World, we love and then think of marriage. Those earlier Victorian marriages were happy many times, and love did come, which ought to give us all the more encouragement in attempting to develop love for those we know would be good for us; but in the final analysis, let's hope that we are also good for them!

One of the concepts that might fit in well here is that of Eric Fromm, who stated that to love somebody is not *just* a strong feeling, it is a decision, it is a judgment, and it is a promise! He goes on to illustrate that feelings come and go, and if love were only a feeling, then there would be no basis for continued love. (*Art of Loving,* p. 14.)

Then, the persistent emotional yearning we have used for a definition, doesn't have to persist every moment of our consciousness, but it persistently finds its way back into our emotions from time to time. When it isn't there we still acknowledge the existence of its reality through our memory of the experience. Thus, memory becomes the life-giving essence of continued love.

It is common for many of us to feel a lot of excited thoughts early in a relationship, but then as we get used to each other and some of the initial intrigue and excitement has disappeared, we wonder if it is still love. It is then that we need to realize our feelings further into a relationship often take on the form of peacefulness and contentment. We feel comfortable with them and enjoy their company, but we don't feel the bad rushes of emotions as frequently. After marriage there is even a sharper increase of this trend. Our love turns more into a commitment. We are not persistently stirred up by the insecurity of wondering if our relationship will last and wondering what the future holds for us. The great anxiousness to win them has been accomplished and we tend to settle back with more of the feelings of security. Again, the memory of our emotions plays a bigger part and our love becomes more one of decision, commitment and promise!

Chapter 6

FALLING OUT OF LOVE

If you are not in the situation that requires you to try to forget someone and stop feeling so much for them, this chapter will not be very important to you at the present time. But hopefully it will give a few helpful suggestions to those trying to deal with a very real problem: forgetting someone with whom they have been emotionally involved.

SENTIMENTAL SLOB

Of all the situations in life, there is nothing that is as emotionally and psychologically involving as dating and loving someone else. We may talk about riches, we may talk about pleasures, but in the hierarchy of human needs we want first to love and be loved. And even beyond love we must first have peace of mind. And when we must break up with someone that we have felt a great deal of love for, it gives us anything but peace of mind!

The amount of time we have gone with the person is a factor, but not a total determinant of how emotionally involved we might be with a person. We can know a person just briefly and the great tugs of emotional desire can remain for many long weeks. If we know them reasonably well and are cut short of fulfilling our emotional desires, the pains of emotional hurt can last for many long months. If we have come to know them for a year or more and have developed great emotional commitments for them and have hopes of marrying them, we are likely to feel the strains of deep disappointment and desire for many long years to come. The imagination of the mind can deepen the emotions of love much faster than time or events.

If you find that it is difficult for you to forget experiences of love, you should know that you have a lot of company. Experiences are related in the newspapers and magazines all the time of those who have been united with a lost love after many long years, or who still have vivid memories of childhood loves even in their old age. Others around you will never appreciate your feelings unless they are suffering through the same situation. Others are likely to say: "Oh, you can forget them if you want to! In a few weeks you won't even remember that they exist." The author would argue with those thoughts! Over a period of time they will become less important to you and you will think of them less often, but if your feelings of love had any real depth to them, you will remember them for a good long period of time.

The writer will relate one personal experience first, which helps to illustrate this point. He had a good friend whom he thought a great deal of and who wanted to date the same girl he was dating, but unbeknown to the writer. Some time later he told the author about it and gave him a little poem that he had written during one of his more emotional moments. He said his feelings about that awkward situation of years before had not dampened in the least. The poem is good enough to print, so here it is:

HAWKE AND THE DOVE

Dashed on the rocks near the land of love,
The wise old Hawke bewildered the Dove
Swooping and swinging in his mental gymnasium,
Hawke made the plan, that put Dove in a dazeium.
He struck hard and fast with swiftness and skill,
Before the slow Dove had determined his will.
Now tranquil, docile and slightly dismayed,
The Dove's flight to the stars will not be delayed.
What the Hawke does now only the future can tell,
As for the Dove, "All is Well," "All is Well."

We never know how we are affecting others around us and what they will remember us for, but one thing we can be sure of is that "Memory" will be there, permanently recording everything that takes place.

There are two excellent stories which illustrate just how long a person remembers. The first concerns the famous American poet, Robert Frost.

ROBERT FROST STORY: In the *Reader's Digest* of August, 1967, Lawrance Thompson, the biographer of Robert Frost, relates the story of a childhood sweetheart of this famous poet. Her name was Sabra Peabody, and as an awkward 12 year-old he wrote her ardent notes, then moved from the town and heard no more about her. The biographer visited this lady when she was in her 70's and found that her memories of Robert Frost where as clear as the poet's had been. On the writer's second visit she related how she had opened an old family trunk in the attic and had found an old wooden pencil box she had used in grammar-school days. She eventually remembered that there was a secret compartment in the bottom of the box. She opened it and out fell four notes written by "Rob" to Sabra. The notes read: "I like those leavs you gave me and put them in my speller to press...." Another note pleaded: "There is no fun in getting mad every so often so lets see if we cant keep friends....I like you because I cant help myself and when I get mad at you I feel mad at myself to." Eventually these notes were put in a vault of the library housing the collection of Robert Frost with a notation: "Not to be opened during Robert Frost's lifetime." On a surprise visit to the vault, Robert Frost found the package, tore it open and read the notes. After reading the notes, he stalked out of the library, leaving the librarian standing there. Later he told the biographer that when he read the notes, a flood of memories swept over him and he could feel the tears burning in his eyes, and so he fled. And then he said, "Sixty years!...and I've never forgotten."

NEW ZEALAND SWEETHEARTS: In a newspaper article the author saw a picture of a couple united after he had walked out on her 53 years earlier. The groom related how they had been going together for a few years, but because of parental interference on both sides, he just ran away from her. He stayed in New Zealand for eleven years and then emigrated to Canada and eventually to the United States. He married twice during those years and both wives died. He tried to get friends in New Zealand to locate his previous sweetheart, but without success. With no clues as to her whereabouts, Mr. Speary took to repeating a simple exercise. When he jumped out of bed every morning he would say aloud, "Rhoda, where are you? Rhoda, where are you?" In the middle of one night he awoke to see in his mind's eye, the words of Rotorua, so he wrote to that community in New Zealand. The card was first stamped "insufficient address," but it did finally reach her. She wrote back saying: "It seems like it's been 2,000 years since I heard from you last." In his third letter, Mr. Speary proposed marriage. He called her long distance after she accepted, and then a travel agency arranged for "red carpet" service for Mr. Speary all the way, with one plane even being called back to pick him up. "It's as if a wound I've had all my life has healed," Mr. Speary said. Mrs. Speary indicated that with every knock of the door for 53 years, she had wondered, "Is that Cyril Speary?" The right knock finally did come and they were married six days later on St. Valentine's Day.

An unusual story, yes! But there are many other unusual stories like it which illustrate with great clarity the truth, that once you have deeply loved a person, you don't forget them entirely. THE EMOTIONS OF LOVE ARE NEVER FORGOTTEN ENTIRELY, THEY ARE JUST PLACED IN A DIFFERENT PERSPECTIVE!

With the two stories that we have just related as a back drop, we are now prepared to launch into the importance of being cautious in the length of time that we spend dating any one given person.

THIEVES OF TIME AND EMOTIONS

One who steals a purse or personal wealth is certainly committing a great evil; but one who steals the emotions of another person and their precious time is a far worse kind of thief. We owe it to our companions to be honest with them!

The writer of this book has encouraged the readers to date more freely, to date more individuals, to stay in circulation, and to take dating a little less seriously. However, this pertains to the earlier stages of dating; after you have dated a person a *half-dozen times,* (more or less) then there should be some real consideration as to your future intentions. If you're still in high school or both understand that marriage isn't a consideration for a long time--then it may not be quite so important. But if either of you are at the age when marriage hopes are a large consideration--then the length and depth of your dating needs to be considered with care and honesty. It may be much too early to talk about the situation together, but it should be considered by each *individually!* Each should ask themselves, "Is this an individual that I could eventually love and marry?" If the answer is a very definite "NO!" then you ought to stop dating immediately. If you know for certain that you couldn't marry the person, you are doing both of you a disservice to continue to date them. Their emotions and hopes will only continue to build, and you have no right to possess their dreams. Not only are you hurting them, you can hurt yourself. Later on it may be harder for you to break it off, and you are robbing them and yourself of precious time that might be spent with someone else who shows much more potential.

There are many cases that are clear cut, but the problem is that most cases are not that definite. There are many gradations, and the author sees at least five major categories of marriage potential:

1. Definitely No!
2. Don't think so; but no one better in sight.
3. Hope so, but still looking!
4. Certain that you want the person, but they aren't certain about you.
5. Both are certain!

It would be wonderful if all of the cases could be definitely No, or definitely Yes. But they aren't, and so the question arises as to "how long" you should permit a relationship to continue with the "indefinite states of existence?" It is impossible to create a meaningful timetable, because every situation is so very different, and many relationships go through an awful lot of time and problems and still end up as happy marriages. In fact, a great deal of love that lasts is slow in its initial development. In addition, there is usually one individual who is slower in deciding about his feelings than the other, and too much impatience could kill a relationship with real potential.

On the other hand, there are too many relationships that go on and on for many long years and only end in bitter disappointment. Everyone would like some kind of a guide line, and so the author will attempt the impossible of presenting one to be considered. The author would challenge the reader to be critical of it and evaluate it differently with each circumstance. It is presented for those who are old enough to be very seriously looking for a marriage partner.

TIMETABLE FOR DATING THAT DOESN'T SEEM TO PROGRESS:

Stage 1:

If you have dated them about four to six times and know you would never marry them, then stop the dating quickly. But if you are not certain, then the following steps might apply.

Stage 2:

After two to three months, you should have talked a little bit about your feelings for each other and what future there might be for the relationship. No definite commitments need to be made, but *some* feeling and understanding of the relationship needs to be established verbally.

Stage 3:

After four to six months of fairly steady-type dating, if it hasn't already been done, there should be some direct efforts made at having some very open conversations about the feelings and intentions of both individuals. Some type of commitments should be evolving from the relationship.

If you aren't thinking about engagements or of going steady soon, then you ought to agree to start dating others as freely as possible. If progress isn't being made, then there ought to be direct efforts to break the relationship.

Stage 4:

After seven to nine months of fairly steady-type dating, if no commitments have been made by then, you should make more serious attempts to stop the relationship or at least agree to see each other just once a month or something; so that both of you can direct your attention at finding someone else that is more promising. You can still be friends, but all effort should be put forth not to permit the relationship to just drag on and on toward the year mark. After you have wasted a year with a person, you may become bitter and feel the other has robbed you of a year of your life.

STEPS OF BREAKING UP

We have in previous chapters discussed problems involved in breaking off a relationship, and a little of what it entails. However, it takes on new light and meaning in view of love and a serious relationship.

There are many reasons why relationships need to be broken up; the following is a list of just a few reasons:

1. We are too young to get involved in a serious relationship.
2. We have too many plans to complete before marriage.
3. We are not impressed that we are in the best company.
4. Our relationship is not a pleasant and happy one.
5. We have someone else that we want to date more seriously.
6. We have been going together too long without making any progress.

The author feels there are about four approaches that should be taken in stopping a relationship.

1. If you haven't dated the person very long, then *just stop* asking or accepting dates. It will do more harm than good to say anything.

2. If you have been dating a person quite steadily for a half-dozen dates, it might be helpful to *taper it off* with one or two more dates spread out over a longer period of time. By tapering, you will still not need to say anything to them, usually.

3. Where you have been dating for a long period of time and where the relationship has been an important one, you need to *talk to the person* and tell them that you don't feel certain about the relationship and that you would like to start dating others more and taper off the relationship with them. Assure them of your friendship for them, and leave the door open to some degree.

4. *Vacation Period Approach:* Some couples feel it helps to start the tapering off by agreeing not to see each other for a period of so many days. Maybe it is a week, or maybe two weeks, and with some even a month, with the understanding that they will see each other again at the conclusion of that period. The advantages of this approach are that you make a definite and complete break, for that period at least. You learn to adjust to the separation at a faster rate. But at the same time you are still assured that you will get together again to visit or date if either party desires it.

GETTING DROPPED YOURSELF!

Emotional reactions are much different when you are the one being dropped. The preceding suggestions are nice when you are contemplating making an end to a serious relationship, since you can plan ahead and get used to the idea. But a shock is coming to you if your dating partner abruptly puts the brakes on what you considered to be a successful relationship! This section, then, is written from the point of view that you are on the losing end and are *not* really in favor of breaking up.

Chances of Saving the Relationship: Your first impulse is usually to try to save the relationship by correcting any areas that need correcting. Some relationships just won't be saved simply because it takes two to tango, and if either individual isn't interested the relationship can't succeed. But assuming that you both would like the relationship to work, then there are at least two major areas that you can work on:

1st: *EXPECTATION LEVELS:* Most relationships go through stages of complications after we have dated for a while, simply because of our expectations! We take into our courtship the idea that men and women have certain things they are supposed to do, and certain ways they are supposed to respond and relate to each other. However, our partner may have an entirely different set of expectation levels from our own. This is one of the reasons it is so important to try to date those of the same cultural and religious backgrounds, to minimize the differences.

The further our relationship develops, the more we begin to depend upon them and the more we begin to expect things out of the relationship. If these things are not forthcoming, we are disappointed and often arguments ensue that make the relationship uncomfortable and create tension. Many times couples are not even really conscious of why they are unhappy with each other. Becoming conscious of these expectation levels can help a great deal in improving our courtship. We can work to fulfill more of their demands. Both parties are probably guilty of expecting too much, and if both will work at tuning these expectations down, many arguments will never begin, and the whole atmosphere of the relationship can greatly improve.

2nd: *PROBLEM SOLVERS vs. PROBLEM CREATORS:* Some people feel there are two kinds of basic personalities: one positive, and one negative; one that is always solving problems, and one that is always creating them. We are usually a combination of both, and we just accentuate or stress one more than the other at various times. It is so easy to become a problem creator in a dating situation. They don't fulfill our expectations, so we challenge our partner on the issues involved, and often we make a bigger deal out of the situation than we should. The issues might be politics, religion, philosophy or any other controversial subjects. Often the issue is of a personal nature, being bothered by something that one of us does or something we fail to do. We continue to talk about it and analyze it to death, or we just stew about it and blow it all out of proportion.

Examine your relationships, can't you see a lot of the above happening? Who is responsible for being the biggest problem creator, you or your partner? What can you do specifically to minimize the acts of "problem creation?" Many relationships go on the rocks simply because there is too little acceptance of small imperfections in each other. We love each other and we are overly zealous to correct and perfect every little aspect of our relationship.

HOW TO BECOME A PEACEMAKER: If you would like to save a relationship that is breaking up, work on the problem-solving aspect, talk to your partner about it and work to develop more tolerance for each other in the little things. As the author's grandmother used to put it: "Don't stir in a mud puddle, you will only make it worse." It is also put another way: "Let sleeping dogs lie." In other words, don't let little things bother you, and don't continue to bring up dead issues. Greet arguments with a smile, with as much agreement as you can, with as few words as possible, and with changing the topic to more positive areas. These suggestions can save a dying relationship, and they can go a long way toward improving any relationship.

HELPS TO FORGETTING

If you have tried your best to save your relationship but failed to do so, or even if you wanted it to end in everyone's best interest but can't get it out of your thoughts, then you are going through one of the loneliest periods in your life. Nonetheless, you must see it through. The author knows what it's like, though, and he has come up with some hints on how to forget, somewhat, the hurt and loss of a past lover.

1. First, make the *Intellectual Decision* to break off the relationship.
2. Next, give *Emotional Acceptance* of the intellectual decision.
3. Have the *Patience* to allow time to heal the wounds and the longings.
4. *Transfer Emotional Dependency* to other people.
5. *Fill the Void* with other activities and involvements.
6. Learn to control *Emotional Inertia* and *Thought Inertia.*
7. Build *Self-image* for future success.

2. *EMOTIONAL ACCEPTANCE:* We have already covered at length the process of making the Intellectual Decision, so next comes the struggle of giving Emotional Acceptance to that decision. We may be very upset with the person, we may be very angry at them and we may even feel some hatred for the person; however, as time passes we will find that we miss them a great deal. Our intellectual decision may be firm, but our emotions cry out for their companionship. The emotional feelings of love are not determined by logic, reasoning, intellectual analysis, mathematical equations or anything along this line. They are simply tender feelings of the heart springing from social interaction with another individual. And it is not easy to change, erase or alter those feelings that jump out at us from the memory of their familiar comfortableness. Many attempt to discount their love and say it wasn't "real love," or it would have lasted and ended in marriage. The author feels this is a dangerous approach, because such individuals will have trouble accepting that they "love" someone else in the future. The feelings for earlier companions return and then they can't give acceptance to the new feelings. It is far too idealistic to feel that a person will only "love" once in life. We will probably never love two people just alike, because love is the mixing of two hearts and personalities together, and we will never respond exactly the same way to any two individuals. *Another person will never completely take the place of our lost lover, but they will take their own rightful place.*

Accepting that you did love the person is an important step in order to forget them, or better put--in order to place them into proper perspective in your memory! Accept the feelings you have felt for them and may still feel for them, but *be firm* in your intellectual decision to find someone else that you can share a new experience of "love" and "feelings" for!

These ideas are best illustrated in a little verse that goes like this:

In the very depth of your soul
Dig a Grave
Let it be as some forgotten spot
To which no path leads

And there in the eternal silence
Bury all of the wrongs that you have suffered.

3. *PATIENCE:* As we attempt to forget the person, it may often seem like it takes forever, and the harder we try to forget, the more longing we experience for them. It seems like there is a strong magnet drawing us back to them, and we cry within for power to demagnitize ourselves from them. But it is like when we burn our finger, the hurt will go away in time if we will just be patient.

Have patience and allow time to heal the wounds and the emotional longings. Likewise, have patience for those you start to date, since they will seem shallow and lacking in depth and personality at first. They won't understand you as the other person seemed to at first.

4. *TRANSFER EMOTIONAL DEPENDENCY:* After we have dated a person for a long period of time and have developed a deep love and appreciation for them, we start to depend on them for a great number of things, and there is created a great emotional dependency for them. We can date others and feel extremely lonely, we can be in a crowd and feel alone; because the only thing that satisfies our emotional needs for company is the person we have grown accustomed to. We felt comfortable with their personality and it seemed to do

something for us. Our emotions are slow to react to our commands to forget them. We must find other objects and other people to take their place. But "things" will not do quite as well as people--we must try to find other people to fill in the vacancy. Best of all, we must *start dating again with others.*

If you are a girl, go out of your way to invite fellows to dinner and get lined up on some blind dates--do anything to get back in circulation. Find someone that gives you some degree of acceptance and keep company with them as much as possible. But don't count on these dates giving you the same fulfillment at first! Next, start spending more time with your family and with other friends. The worst thing you can do is sit home and stew over your loneliness; get out and mix with all the people you can. You must attempt to place as much of that emotional dependency on other people as you can.

5. *FILL THE VOID:* If we have developed a deep love for a person, we must have spent a great deal of time with them. Again, we must fill that void with meaningful activities. We must become busier than we have ever been before.

Get physically involved in sports, hobbies and projects. Play a musical instrument, paint a picture, or do some creative writing. Become engrossed in an area of study or skill that you particularly enjoy. *The unhappy people in this world are those who don't have many secondary involvements to fall back on when their primary involvement meets with disaster.* Have you ever noticed how some people seem to have a lot of tragedies in their lives and yet they are often much happier than those who never seem to have any major problem confront them? It is all in how they take it. Usually speaking, the *same things happen to happy people as happen to unhappy people--it is just how they take it.* They develop a healthy attitude toward life and the things that happen in it. So if you feel miserable because you are trying to break up with a person you have dated for a long time, keep these thoughts in mind. You must become excited about your life and specifically with what you are doing to keep your mind occupied. Until you are as emotionally involved with other people and activities as you were with your friend, you will not completely win the battle of placing the lost lover in the proper place in your memory.

6. *LEARN TO CONTROL THOUGHT INERTIA:* The law of inertia is that a body at rest tends to remain at rest, and a body in motion tends to remain in motion. And the same goes for our thought patterns. If our thoughts tend to be lazy and unproductive, they will tend to remain that way. If our thoughts tend to be active and creative, they will tend to remain such. And if our thoughts tend to be dwelling on our lost love, then they will remain on them. LIKE THOUGHTS GATHER SIMILAR AND LIKE THOUGHTS!

We may drive by a place that involved one of our dates and that reminds us of our old lover, then we think of other dates we had, and we continue to gather one thought after another. Our "thought inertia" gathers speed and likewise does our "emotional inertia," and soon we are depressed and discouraged and lonely for them. We hear a special song that we both liked, and off goes our "emotional memory" into other experiences that involved us. The longer we permit these thoughts to gather, the more difficult it seems to put on the brakes.

Realizing that like thoughts breed more thoughts of the same nature can be a great help in attempting to forget a person. When you catch yourself thinking about them, exert all of your efforts to control your thought patterns into another direction. Concentrate on something else, ask yourself some questions in a different area entirely. Talk to someone else with enough enthusiasm to divert your attention from the person you are attempting to forget. Control your Thought Inertia!

7. *BUILD SELF-IMAGE FOR FUTURE SUCCESS:* Along with controlling our thoughts and diverting them away from past memories, we should try to divert our thought patterns into very positive channels that build confidence in ourselves. As we concentrate on believing in ourselves and our own self-worth, we will automatically become worth more in the eyes of others. We will become a more valuable prospect in our future dating cycles and also in other things we do in life. As we believe in our own self-worth, we will be less likely to be intimidated by those who don't accept us as a dating companion. We will be less likely to be hurt and will find it easier to forget

those who reject us. Believing in yourself, then, is an important step to forgetting lost lovers.

It may help to summarize some of the preceding ideas and place them on a card. Then you can carry the card with you or place it on walls where you spend most of your time. The author made one such little card that went like this:

DO YOU FEEL YOU ARE GETTING DISCOURAGED?

1. *Then get excited about life! Do it quickly!*
2. *When a discouraging thing happens--think quickly about your successes!*
3. *Concentrate on your affirmations!*

Simply put, affirmations are things that you confirm positively to yourself or tell yourself that you would like. A successful person makes a list of things he wants and he continually affirms them in his mind and gathers more thoughts to help them become realities.

With this list or one like it as a constant reminder, you should be able to more easily conquer your depressions and anxieties. Anything will become easier to do as you work at it, even falling out of love! Remember that *love is not limited to once per customer, per lifetime!* If you have experienced love, you are actually better off, for you have felt its reality and you know you are capable of feeling great emotions for another human being. Chances are even better that you will experience it again in the future.

If the reader is interested in more thoughts along the line of controlling your mind and planning the success of your life, you may be interested in another book compiled by this author entitled: *Art of Achieving Success.* Also, in Chapter 9 of this book we will discuss these concepts in more detail, and analyze the development of the personality.

Chapter 7

WHY BE MORAL?

There are many who feel there are no good reasons to be sexually moral any more. Ideas of sexual freedom are becoming more accepted by young people, and the sacred institution of marriage is being scoffed and ridiculed as meaningless--at least, so it would seem. We will first list some of the reasons people give for being "immoral," and then we will give some reasons for being moral.

REASONS TO BE IMMORAL

1. *Physical Desire:*
   I feel the strong physical urges to be immoral, they are natural and need to be fulfilled.
2. *Curiosity:*
   I am very curious to know what it will be like; just once won't hurt.
3. *Popularity:*
   Everyone else is doing it, I will not be popular if I don't, and I will lose my present dating companion. I am lonely. It is the way you prove your love for them.
4. *Rebelliousness:*
   I resent my parents and society and get tired of their dictations. I want to prove that I am a *free agent* and prove my independence. I have been rejected by previous lovers--I will show them! I am discouraged with life's treatment of me, why not do whatever I feel like doing?

There are endless other reasons given, but most of them can be categorized into one of these four areas. These reasons are very logical to many people, especially when they are looking for excuses to justify their conduct. Now let's take each of these reasons and briefly analyze them to see just how logical they really are.

PHYSICAL DESIRE & CURIOSITY:

Every human being is possessed with the physical desires toward the opposite sex. They were put there for the preservation of the human race. The element of curiosity of the unknown, combined with the sexual desire, is a very driving force. And it doesn't help when myths are created around sex which imply that "sex is everything." The implication is that sex is the answer to all of your problems whether they are sexual in nature or not. When everything is connected to sex, it becomes difficult to determine and appreciate those areas that are truly sexual. So, youngsters grow up with a distorted view of sex and what sex will do for them. Young people are often enticed into the sex-trap to find release for their tensions, their loneliness, and their insecurities, only to find that sex has solved nothing, but only complicated each of their problems to a greater extent. Sexual indulgence will destroy peace, happiness and self-respect. We will go more into this area later.

Sex Drives are an Appetite: One should understand that sexual drives are an appetite of the body. Many feel that just once won't hurt and may satisfy their urge. But this is like getting a small bite of a watermelon center and pretending that you don't want any more. And even when you have filled yourself with watermelon, this doesn't do away with the desire to eat it again. Eating a meal does not do away with your desire to ever eat again. It is merely temporary satisfaction. And so it is with your sexual drives; participating in just a little sexual play will only make you want to go further. And even if you could satisfy your urges for the day, those urges will return very rapidly. The fact that you have already indulged makes it so much easier to do in the future. It all started with "just once won't hurt," rationale, and then after the once is over, your rationale changes to the idea that once more certainly won't make any difference, because you have already done it once. The best way to attack the problem is to never get involved. Wait until after marriage!

Understanding that the sexual desire is an appetite can often help in controlling it. Another concept that may help to realize is that physiologically, *we cannot possess pleasure; pleasure possesses us.* It exists in the body as pure sensation in the moment of happening, independent of our will. As soon as the body comes under the conscious control of the mind, pleasure ends. Considering these physical facts, people would be wise to realize that giving vent to their physical desires will not give them the lasting release and pleasure they may have contemplated. It would be wiser to seek happiness, and happiness only comes from obeying moral laws. While pleasure is only a temporary sensation, happiness can be a more lasting possession.

POPULARITY:

Those attempting to promote the world of sex and sell materials that arouse the sexual appetite are continuously attempting to convince the world that everyone else is doing it. You can read endless opinion polls that have been taken by authors, newspapers and the smallest amateurs that suggest all kinds of percentages of those who have indulged in sexual activities. Their percentages vary so greatly that it is obvious their samples are not scientifically selected to produce an honest picture. In fact, one wonders if their samples may be "scientifically" selected to produce just the kind of picture they would like the public to believe! The more objective and comprehensive reports, like the Kinsey Report and other more recent studies, have found that the large majority are *not* indulging in sexual activity. The degenerates, however, either ignore these studies, or if they are confronted with them, they don't talk about the many who are not involved--they just focus in on how many are indulging. They seek to justify their indulgence by preferring to believe that all are as animalistic and miserable as themselves, or they talk about the "new morality" and try to justify their actions on the new trends.

There is nothing new about the "new morality." All generations have contained small groups who have been proclaiming that their generation is different, and therefore not bound by old traditions of morality. The truth of the matter is that everybody is *NOT* doing it; it might be more accurate to say, "many are talking about it." Often the ones who are doing the talking are the loud ones, the obnoxious and crude ones. These are the persons who don't respect the rights of others and hold few things sacred. They may not know what they're talking about, but they certainly get a lot of public attention.

Will be dropped: If your present dating companions demand sexual privileges as their price for dating you, then the price is too great, and you are better off without them. And this goes for popularity with others, if this is their demand. This is not the price of popularity as so many would have you believe, unless you are keeping company with only the degenerates. The majority do not require such privileges, and so in worthwhile company, popularity has nothing to do with your sexual permissiveness.

Lonely: If you feel lonely and think that this is a justified reason for sexual looseness, wait until after you have involved yourself sexually with someone, and they suddenly drop you--your loneliness then will far exceed anything you have experienced. Can you imagine what you would feel like to give your body to someone, only to have them make light of you with others and drop you flat? This happens every day the world goes around; don't think your case will be so different!

Test of your love: One of the oldest lines ever given for trying to weaken you and make you feel you should submit to demands is: "If you really loved me, you would." This is about as phony as you can get--there was never a bigger lie. In a mature, genuine and meaningful love, you desire what is best for the other individual and you would never want to hurt them in any way. And when you ask a person to engage in the sex act before marriage, you are hurting them in more ways than you can imagine. You hurt their own self-image, their image of you, you risk hurting their reputation with others, and you may risk getting them in trouble with an unexpected child. There are endless ways in which you hurt them, but the ramifications of this kind of involvement are never very evident until it's too late. Remember, wise love is kind and wholesome. To love is to give, not take. To love is to serve, not to exploit.

Some extremists go as far as to say that if someone wants sexual freedom with you, there could not possibly be any "love" present. The author would rather state it in the terms stated above: there must not be any "mature, genuine and meaningful love" present. They might feel some real love for the person, but they also have *Lust!* And love is not lust, nor is lust, love. The writer feels it is important to realize that there can be some differences between *lust* and *love.* It would be possible to love a person and feel a great anxiousness to be married to them and desire sexual association with them to the point that you might describe it as "lust." So on these grounds, a person could feel some genuine feelings for you and also feel so much "physical attraction" and lust that they submit to their baser nature and attempt to convince you to indulge in activities that are not for the best good of either of you. And when they do this, they are not demonstrating a mature, genuine and meaningful love for you. They may be misinformed as to proper conduct in love. When and if they question your love for them, you really have more meaningful grounds to question their love for you!

Meaningful love doesn't have to be proven with submission; it is proven by acceptance of a person for what they are, and what they have already been to you, without further unreasonable demands. Love is so much more significant when there are evidences that you seek your partner's complete happiness, comfort, and well-being, and when you attempt to elevate the person into doing the right things, wholesome things, and things that they will never have to regret! In a mature love you may feel some strong feelings of physical desire, but you overrule and control them because of your genuine concern for your partner's happiness, and because the sincerity of your love is so intense that you would do nothing which would spoil or damage the high quality of your love for them. You become a protector and not a molestor.

If you have illusions that popularity will be yours from sexual promiscuity, you will find yourself popular only as the prostitute that you have really become, by so submitting yourself. You will find yourself losing meaningful popularity with respectable and high quality companions that could bring genuine happiness to your life. When you give of your body to prove your love, you have given no more than any other prostitute gives. Really, the only thing that is ever "proven" is that you have poor judgement, that you are weak-willed, that you have no self-mastery or character, and that you are carnal and lust after the things of the flesh.

REBELLIOUSNESS:

There are some young people who get themselves into trouble morally, simply because they resent their parents and society telling them what to do. They are out to prove that they are "FREE" and that they will do as they please. Those who use this reasoning for violating sexual codes are probably using some of the most childish reasons they could ever think up. They are naive and have not learned a basic and simple truth that *Freedom carries with it Responsibility!* You are only free until you act, and after you act you are responsible for those decisions made under the guise of freedom. For example, you are free to drink poison, but after you have acted you must pay the consequences. You are free to drive your car off a cliff, but after you have acted you forfeit any freedom to reverse the consequences. A man and woman are free to commit the sex act, but afterwards the woman can no longer call herself a virgin, and the man can claim no virginity. They have broken trust with their families, with each other, with their religious teachings and with the ethical code of any community. They can no longer claim to be clean and pure from violating a sacred command of their Father in Heaven. They have hurt their parents, they have hurt others who are concerned for them and they have hurt themselves. What have they gained by calling themselves free? What are they now free of? They are now free of being 100 percent worthy of someone else who has kept himself "bound" by the structure of rules and laws. Rules and laws are simply guide lines to help us find more happiness in life and to protect us from painful pitfalls. We can rebel against society all we want, but if we fail to heed the advice of experience, we are doomed to pay the price of our mistakes.

> *It is a wise person that learns by experience, but a wiser person that learns from the experiences of others.*
>
> *And those that will not learn from history are doomed to repeat the mistakes of the past.*

TEN REASONS TO REMAIN VIRTUOUS

We have already covered several good reasons to remain virtuous in the previous section; however, in this section we will organize them into a more logical sequence of ten major reasons:

1. For the sake of your children.
2. For your own self-respect.
3. For the sake of your parents.
4. For the sake of respecting your date.
5. For the sake of your future spouse.
6. For the protection against disease.
7. For the sake of your mental health.
8. For the sake of Society.
9. Because it is a command of God.
10. So that you can grow spiritually.

So many who get themselves into trouble are defiant towards everyone else, and often make statements like the following: "I am a free agent, what I do shouldn't concern anyone else. If I choose to get involved sexually with someone, that is my business and I won't be hurting anyone but myself!" A statement of this nature is so naive that it is difficult to believe that anyone could be so unaware of how their life affects others around them. You will be affecting at least *three generations* and probably many more. First your child, then yourself, and then your parents.

WHY BE MORALLY CLEAN?

1st: *REMAIN MORAL FOR THE SAKE OF YOUR CHILDREN:* This reason is logically first because the real purpose of sex is to have children. The complete joys of sexual union cannot be experienced through just the selfish pleasures of the flesh, but through the seeking of its natural objective, that of desiring children within a marriage.

We have a responsibility to our unborn children that is real and significant. The girl is the one that is more directly involved, but it is equally the responsibility of the father. Those babies have a right to a fair deal, which means they have a right to have parents who are devoted to each other, and who want them and who are prepared to have them. So many girls are duped into believing that the man they are having an affair with will marry them. They receive endless promises that are immediately forgotten when the girl announces that she is expecting. Many fellows run off and join the military, and others just disappear rather than face the music of providing a proper home for the coming child.

With freedom comes responsibility, and if you are going to take the "freedom" to indulge in sexual relations, you have the "responsibility" to be married first! And if you don't have the character to realize that, then hopefully you will if a child does come on the scene; but girls had better not count on it whatsoever. Shotgun marriages of this variety have a drastically high mortality rate of ending in divorce. And what chance does a child have in a divided home? Courts over the land have time and again related the vast majority of juvenile delinquency to broken homes. Again, what chance does the child have, are they being given a fair break? The man usually pays the smallest price, the woman pays the next highest price, but the child pays the most!

Maybe you don't think your immoral decision is anybody else's business and that only you suffer, but it just isn't so.

You have no right to ever create a potential situation where an unborn child will have to pay a price later on for your stupidity.

Birth Control Devices: Many indicate that there doesn't need to be any unwanted children any more because of the various birth control devices, and now there is even legalized abortion. But the cases are endless of times when there are slip-ups with every one of the methods, and the "unwanted children" still arrive in their "unwanted environment." And certainly no sane person would consider abortion, legalized or not, as an alternative. There are too many disadvantages, including cost, danger to health, and a guilty conscience.

When children do come and grow up and need your counsel to remain moral, will you be qualified for the task? The paradox is that we will demand things of our children that we may not have been equal to ourselves! If the children ever find out that their parents were immoral, and they or others were conceived out of wedlock, they can often develop complexes and poor attitudes about their own conduct in regards to morals and other laws of society. Your children can pass on to their children the same poor attitudes and it can be carried on for many generations to come--and all of this can begin with some little whimsical desire to experiment and to satisfy a selfish desire for momentary pleasure, at the expense of an unborn child.

2nd: *REMAIN MORAL FOR YOUR OWN SELF-RESPECT:* There are few things that are more important in life than being able to live with yourself. If you are unhappy with yourself, disappointed in yourself, then your whole world is affected. We succeed in life because of the faith we have in ourselves. We find happiness because of our attainments and because we know that we have done our best in life. Everyone knows deep down that immorality is wrong. The power to love another rests on the ability to respect oneself.

The writer has known some of the most crude men in the world who would brag of their sexual conquests in public, but who would, in more solemn moments alone with the author, confess to the fact that they knew there must be something wrong with it, and that they felt they lost something every time they engaged in immorality. They found it harder to look others in the eye. They found that they were disqualified to date certain types of people that they felt were moral. They often began to question their ability to do a lot of things, just because they failed to keep faith with themselves and to live on the level they knew they should.

As a young man doing religious work, the author once witnessed an elderly lady in her late seventies break down into tears while teaching her the Gospel. She told of how she had once acted foolishly as a girl. It was a great lesson to the writer, because it illustrated that once you act foolishly in regards to morals--you never forget and you often find it difficult to completely forgive yourself the rest of your life, even though you should. One of the real tests of man's creation is his ability to control his appetites and direct them into the right channels of marriage. Those who do not maintain self-restraint have proven themselves losers in life. They are without character and untrue to themselves.

More and more college youth are accepting their so-called "sexual freedom" to mean they are also *free to remain moral.* They pity those of their number who plunge into promiscuity to express their freedom. You often hear such things as, "'Poor kid, she (or he) is so insecure.'" They realize sexual involvement is a sign of insecurity and a lack of self-confidence, which produces submission to sex for any kind of acceptance that can be achieved.

3rd: *REMAIN MORAL FOR THE SAKE OF YOUR PARENTS:* Acts of immorality are usually surrounded by gross selfishness, and ingratitude is one of the worst kinds of selfishness. Parents give much of their lives for the benefit of their children, and they often sacrifice a great deal for the comfort of their children. In actual cash expense, the average family spends about $15,000 before a child takes off on his own. And if they should pay for his college education, there could be another $5,000 or more. Depending on the income of the family, some may spend less, but many will spend much more.

To this should be added the pains and discomforts that a mother has in carrying a child for nine months and the pains of childbearing. Many mothers spend a good eight hours a day specifically with their new babies, but for the sake of averages, let's just credit her with four hours a day for the period of the first five years of the child's life. This would equal 1500 hours a year, or 7500 hours in five years. Then during the next fifteen years, let's just figure an average of two hours per child per day, or about 750 hours per year, and 11,250 hours for the fifteen years; with a grand total of 18,750 hours. Many of these good mothers left good paying jobs as nurses and school teachers, and other jobs where they were earning as much as $5.00 an hour. If they had stayed on these jobs for many years they could probably have made considerably more. But let's just use a real conservative figure over these years of only $4.00 an hour. This would mean that the average mother would have invested in her child the sum of *$75,000* worth of time! But our averages are probably too conservative. Maybe we ought to give the father credit for some time also, and if we figured that in along with actual expenses, we would probably easily exceed $100,000 dollars. Do you feel worth $100,000 dollars? Some parents have thought so much of their children that they have paid that much again in ransom money. And the money isn't the important thing, it is the deep emotional involvement they have invested.

Well, maybe you are your own boss, maybe you are a free agent, maybe no one is going to tell you what you can do or can't do. And really, your parents want you to stand on your own two feet. However, if you have even an ounce of gratitude in your soul, you should feel some responsibility to honor your parents. *"Honour thy father and thy mother: that thy days may be long upon the land which the Lord thy God giveth thee!"* (Exodus 20:12.)

How do you honor your parents? You do things that would bring them respect and honor. You keep yourself honorable and respectful in any way imaginable. Whether you personally agree with the ethical codes of society or not, you honor your parents by living according to them. You remain honest in every way possible, you abide by the laws of the land

and the laws of God. Anyone who thinks he can honor his parents through immorality must have a head full of sand! Your parents don't want the $100,000 investment back; all they want is your happiness and success in life! They want to look at you and be proud of the character you have developed in doing the right things in life.

Along with this third reason should be mentioned *Grandparents.* Grandparents often feel as anxious as your own parents for you to succeed in doing the right things. And then there are hosts of others in your life that spend time teaching you and helping you to succeed. When you break the ethical codes of morality, you let a whole group of people down, who were pulling for you to make it in life.

4th: *REMAIN VIRTUOUS FOR THE SAKE OF RESPECTING YOUR DATE:* Paths have ways of crossing many times throughout life. You may figure that you may never see your date again and so it doesn't matter what you do with them; but as sure as you take that approach you will find yourself meeting again in unforeseen circumstances. It is always a happier meeting when you can look each other in the eye and know you have nothing to be ashamed of.

One of the driving forces to encourage a person toward marriage is the desire to enjoy sexual activity; if you permit this before marriage, you have nullified a major reason to get married. Also, the chances of a girl having a child from immorality are ever present no matter what precautions may be taken. It can affect and change the girl's life for an entire year at least, and indirectly affect the rest of her life. Every crude fellow who treats the sex act as a pleasure game ought to be sentenced by a judge to live for nine months in close relationship with a girl expecting a child! Observing the morning sickness and other discomforts, and then actually observing the drama of birth is an eye-opening experience. It may not affect or change some hardened playboys, but the author feels it might change a great number of others and cause many to appreciate why societies the world over have established moral codes. If you respect your date at all, you certainly would want them to retain their virtue and peace of mind.

5th: *REMAIN VIRTUOUS FOR THE SAKE OF YOUR FUTURE SPOUSE:* The term "future spouse" may seem like a very distant concept and rather inconceivable at the moment, but rest assured that it will become important in time. And if you have not remained virtuous and should fall in love with someone who has retained his virtue, you will feel somewhat unworthy of that person and deeply regret that you cannot offer him the same purity he offers you. When the person finds out, he or she will think less of you, that is if they will accept you at all. Dr. Terman of Stanford concluded that the more sexually promiscuous a man or woman is before marriage, the less likely they are to be happy in marriage.

Marriage is based upon commitment, a total commitment to each other; and the love and happiness of the marriage is based upon honoring the marriage agreement. There is a loyalty and trust level that enriches the relationship. If there is an awareness that a partner was immoral before marriage, there will always be reasons to wonder and question their moral character after marriage. They may be 100 percent loyal, but the individual is always open to more suspicion. It just adds to the joy of the marriage commitment to know that there has not been that emotional and physical commitment with others.

6th: *REMAIN VIRTUOUS FOR PROTECTION FROM DISEASE:* A person doesn't have to read many newspapers to realize that diseases contracted through the sex act are on the increase all of the time. Venereal Disease (VD) in its various forms is now considered an epidemic and is out of hand. One article estimates that 2800 persons catch this dreaded disease every day in the United States. Similar articles also talk about gonorrhea and syphilis cases reaching epidemic proportions. Many are mislead into thinking that these diseases are under control in our modern medical world, but the U.S. Public Health Service reports V.D. is the Nation's leading Communicable Disease. Syphilis is a killer; it maims, causes heart trouble, insanity and blindness. Gonorrhea isn't much nicer. These diseases are not talked about very much, because even the most vulgar person would prefer that it isn't known that they are so diseased. So they become "silent diseases."

To illustrate the importance of this topic, it might be meaningful to give descriptions of the pain and suffering that many undergo when they so innocently contract these diseases from a few foolish moments of letting down their guard and becoming involved sexually. However, the author has felt that he would rather not have those morbid details in the book. He would prefer to mention the fact that Venereal Disease is very easy to catch and stress that this is another major reason to remain virtuous! The chances of contracting the disease for yourself alone are not worth it; but it becomes even more important that you don't contract the disease and pass it on to your eventual marriage partner. And of course there are the possibilities of birth defects in your unborn children, which would be something that you could never forgive yourself for the rest of your life. Therefore, remain virtuous, if for no other reason than to protect yourself and others from disease!

7th: *REMAIN VIRTUOUS TO RETAIN YOUR MENTAL HEALTH & PEACE OF MIND:* It so often appears that those who engage in sex so freely are not bothered by their actions in the least. They seem so carefree and unconcerned about the consequences of their actions. It is very possible that many of them are totally unconcerned and very little affected by their own actions, and that they will never be affected, but it is more likely that they *will* be affected at some time in their life. Most people in the world who are honest with themselves find great peace in living virtuously, or on the other hand, the lack of peace from non-virtuous living. Many people feel condemned for their sex practices and suffer varying degrees of depression. They regret deeply not waiting until they were married, or in the case that they were already married, they bitterly regret not remaining faithful to their marriage partners. Many lives become deeply affected by divorce, as a result of someone not remaining faithful. Broken homes, broken families, longing desires, deep hatreds and even murders are so very often related to unfaithfulness. Many break under the pressure, have nervous breakdowns and suffer varying degrees of mental illness. It is often the case that those in mental hospitals can trace their history back to sexual involvements.

May this writer add quickly that *there are many other causes of mental illness* and one should not misconstrue this writing to infer that all cases are so related.

But the fact that many mental health cases are related to sex is evidenced by the great influence that Freud was able to have in Psychology, by relating sex to people's problems. Much of modern day Psychology is based upon Freudian influence, which attempts to free people from the guilty feelings they have for sex involvements and other wrong doings. The whole approach of many psychologists is based upon the theory that if they can convince people that they are not responsible for their social actions, or that their actions were not that wrong--then they will free themselves from guilt and they will return to sound mental health. In these kinds of cases they may have found the cause for the ill-health, but their remedy is just the opposite of what it should be!! Today many psychologists are turning away from this approach. One of these men is Dr. O. Hobart Mowrer, former President of the American Psychological Assn. He writes: "We have good reason to believe that psychopathology, instead of stemming from inexpressed sex and hostility, comes rather from an outraged conscience and a violated sense of human decency and responsibility."

The way this whole thing really works is this. Every individual born into this world is born with the "Spirit of Christ," which is the spirit of light and truth; many people choose to call it their "conscience." Whatever you choose to call it, everyone has within them a natural gift and awareness of right and wrong. There are so many things of a moralistic nature that you don't have to be told are right or wrong, you just intuitively know! You don't have to be taught by a preacher that total sexual involvement outside of marriage is wrong--there is something down deep that whispers forth that it is not good.

Now being aware of the fact that a person has the Spirit of Christ within them, it logically follows that when we go against this common sense feeling, we lose the spirit of "peace" within us. We long for the return of that peace, but it evades us until we are willing to pay the price. What is the price? It is not the approach of many modern psychologists to justify our actions; but just the opposite--that of *acknowledging that we did wrong!*

It is all-consumingly important that you confess to your error, your sin or whatever you choose to call it. Confess it to yourself, confess it to your God in prayer, and confess it to any others who may have been directly offended and personally involved. If you have a religious leader who needs to know about these kinds of things, according to your belief, then it would also be important to confess your error to him, in order to be right with your religion and completely free in your mind that you have cleared these actions with everyone that really needs to know. It is not necessary to confess your error in front of everyone; in fact it would be very unwise to broadcast it to everyone. No one needs to know except those who are directly involved or offended. Confession is good for the soul! It is not easy to confess; it is easier at first to listen to the liberal society and learned psychologists who would try to free your mind of guilt by mere verbal pronouncements. But final and conclusive relief will only come when you are big enough to completely admit that you were wrong and that you did wrong and turn away from the actions altogether in the future! Then and only then can you regain peace of mind. At this point you must believe that you have repented and that you will be forgiven. It is important to *forgive yourself!* If you believe that God will forgive, who are you, not to also forgive yourself?

So in conclusion, you can repent and regain peace of mind once again, but the road to regaining that peace is not easy! It would be so much better if you could always remain virtuous! For this reason alone, it would be well worth your while to remain virtuous, to retain your mental health and peace of mind.

> *Though your sins be as scarlet,*
> *they shall be as white as snow.* (Isaiah 1:18.)

8th: *REMAIN VIRTUOUS FOR THE GOOD OF THE COMMUNITY:* Can you imagine what your community would be like if 100 percent of the people were involved in sexual violations with each other? There would be no family ties, no genuine love for each other, because genuine love demands loyalty. Think of the disease that would be infested in everyone. There would be no stability to the community at all, there would be a total breakdown in all of civilization and everything would fall apart. It has actually happened on a smaller scale throughout history. The fall of Rome and Sodom and Gomorrah are well-known examples of the consequences of moral decay. It just stands to reason that there needs to be some moral standards for the good of society in general. And if it is good for society in general, then it ought to be good enough for each of us individually! The degree that we fall individually will be the degree to which our society also falls.

9th: *REMAIN VIRTUOUS BECAUSE IT IS A COMMAND OF GOD!* For those who believe in God, the reason that God has commanded it should be enough. God said through his apostle Paul, that those who commit adultery and fornication should not inherit the kingdom of God. (Galatians 5:19-21) In another chapter Paul also said that we should not keep company with fornicators. (I Cor. 6:9-13)

Adultery, by definition, is where individuals are married and commit the sex act with someone other than their marriage partner. Fornication generally refers to those committing the sex act before marriage.

The Bible is filled with exhortations to chastity and virtue, and condemnations of immorality. Just a few of the references to God's commandment to keep ourselves clean are: (I Peter 2:11) *"Abstain from fleshly lusts, which war against the soul."*

(II Timothy 2:22) *"Flee youthful lusts."*

(Matt. 5:27-28) *"Whosoever looketh on a woman to lust after her hath committed adultery with her already in his heart."*

(Gen. 39:7-13) *One of the classic scriptural stories on this subject, concerning Joseph of old, who was tempted by the Pharoah's wife and who fled from her!*

The scriptures are most clear on this matter. Those who are good God-fearing individuals know this and find this reason enough to remain virtuous--God hath commanded it.

10th: *REMAIN VIRTUOUS THAT YOU MAY GROW SPIRITUALLY:* This reason is closely tied in with the previous one. Sex, combined with love and spirituality in a marriage relationship, form an exalting and intricate interaction which increases the significance of each ingredient to indescribable proportions. Conversely, outside of marriage, sex formulates a destroying force which mutilates and severs true love and spirituality. There are probably no two things which are more diametrically opposed than "spirituality" and "adulterated sex."

If you know you are not obeying the commands of God, you cannot hope for His spirit to be with you. Those who do not restrain their sexual appetites will often admit that they feel like they lose something, but they are not always sure what it is. One of the things they lose is spirituality. The things of God are not discerned by the reasoning and intellect of man, but by the Spirit of God, whose influence dwells within man to enable him to perceive spiritual things.

This concept is illustrated very well in I Cor. 2:11-13:

> *For what man knoweth the things of a man, save the spirit of man which is in him? even so the things of God knoweth no man, but the Spirit of God. Now we have received, not the spirit of the world, but the spirit which is of God; that we might know the things that are freely given to us of God. Which things also we speak, not in the words which man's wisdom teacheth, but which the Holy Ghost teacheth; comparing spiritual things with spiritual.*

Those who have not sought after the "spiritual realm" will not understand what we are talking about here, for it is an entirely different experience than many worldly individuals have ever come in contact with. It is a peaceful assurance that comes to those who attempt to live righteously and obey all of God's commandments in humility and with much prayer. The author has felt the spirit of the Lord many times and would encourage the whole world to seek after it! The joy of living is increased so many times and life becomes meaningful and right. Only fools partake of the spirit of the Lord and then cut themselves from it by unvirtuous living. For a few brief moments of physical pleasure some foolish individuals indulge and thus sever themselves from continuing joy and peace, that comes from knowing that you are at least doing some very important things right.

We all have physical desires and have moments when we are strongly drawn toward sexual thoughts and desire sexual experience. We need not think we are evil because of these most natural inclinations. God put these desires there that we might marry and continue our race. Involving ourselves in the sex act within marriage has nothing to do with decreasing spirituality; but outside of the marriage covenant it has everything to do with destroying spirituality. And if a person is ever to find spirituality again, after violating the sex law, it can only be through total repentance and turning away from sexual involvements with others.

When you feel the spirit of the Lord you are at peace with the world, and often you feel the spirit of conviction and testimony. It burns within your heart and tells you more assuredly than earthly reasoning that God is real, and that He does indeed have a divine plan for us to follow! The joy of these experiences is reason enough to remain virtuous--so that you might continue to grow spiritually!

Sex Thoughts: Controlling one's thoughts is always very difficult, but the thoughts that are the most difficult of all to control are those which deal with sex. For a single person, they seem to loom out at times as a power beyond human ability to contain. The more room you give these kinds of thoughts, the harder they are to contain; while the more you control them, the easier they are to minimize! The answer is contained in the little line, oft repeated in this book: "Like thoughts gather like thoughts!" If you fill your mind with ideas about sex, your mind will be as a magnet in gathering more of the same kind of thoughts. Fill your mind with despondency and depression and you will find that your mind gathers more of the same. Fill your mind with positiveness and happiness and you will tend to gather more of the same kind of thoughts. So, the secret to controlling your mind about sex is to keep your mind busily occupied with other things.

If you are not going to try to work at the concept of having a pure mind, then ask yourself the following question: "Just where is it you plan to stop?" Just how far down the line do you plan to go? *Remember, you are becoming what you are thinking!* You cannot travel within and stand still without. If your inner thoughts are constantly upon evil, if your mind is dominated by lustful thoughts, then you will eventually seek their reality in the flesh. "As a Man thinketh, so is he!"

As James Allen has put it, "Men imagine that thought can be kept secret, but it cannot, it ultimately reveals itself in our speech and actions. A noble and Godlike character is not a thing of favour or chance, but is the natural result of continued effort in right thinking, the effect of long cherished association with Godlike thoughts."

PREVENTATIVE MEASURES

How do we keep ourselves virtuous? What preventative measures can be taken? The following guide lines are given in hopes of challenging the reader to think in the area of prevention. Hopefully the reader can come up with many more preventative measures of their own:

1. Girls should keep themselves well-clothed! Wear attractive clothing, but it shouldn't be sexually appealing to the unpealing point. Suggestive and daring dress does more to encourage immorality than anything else.
2. Avoid "making out" sessions that cause excessive stimulation and don't end.
3. Keep your hands where they belong; never venture even for a moment onto areas which are private to a person!
4. Keep your hands from ever going under your date's clothing. The first inch may be so innocent and without

any error, but the problem is that the first inch so innocently becomes two inches and more.

5. Double date as much as you can, and avoid being alone in places which are too private.
6. Avoid staying out too late alone. Keep reasonable hours. Either party can suggest certain hours that they ought to be in by and work toward it.
7. Avoid traveling too long of distances without meaningful chaperones.
8. Never stay together alone overnight, even if you are fully dressed.
9. On overnight camp-outs with many mixed individuals--make a special effort to separate the sexes with a clear-cut demarcation line. We have sometimes referred to it as the "DMZ Demilitarized Zone."
10. If you feel the sexual drives stirring up too often and too greatly--you should change your dating pattern quickly! Very likely you should either get married to the person very soon or you should stop dating them.
11. Guard against the rationalizations that creep in as you get more serious. It doesn't matter what others are doing, or how great your love is, there is still no reason to rationalize your standards away.
12. Avoid conversation that fringes upon the sexual areas and don't joke about it in any way. Keep sex a "sacred area" that is not joked about. Jokes often lead into seriousness; some tell them as feelers to see how their partner will react before becoming more aggressive. Be pleasant but firm in keeping such topics off limits.
13. Keep company with those you know without question you can trust. If there is any doubt, drop them immediately! Also, double date with company that thinks as you do about the area of sexual involvements.
14. Avoid movies and activities that are highly suggestive of sexual thoughts and activities.
15. Keep yourselves busily engaged in wholesome and positive areas. Keep your body and mind engaged in positive areas. If you would stay pure, you must begin with controlling your mind--actions are preceded by thoughts.

If you are a girl and find yourself in a situation where a fellow is forcefully trying to go all the way, and you find that you are not physically strong enough to stop him, you may have one last resort. That is, remain rational and keep talking to the man; ask him questions, try to get him to say something, and it will often make it impossible for him to remain sexually active.

In conclusion then, there are many good reasons to be moral, and there are many preventative steps we can take to protect morality. But much of what has been said can be summed up into one key:

KEY 19: TO BE SUCCESSFUL IN DATING—REMAIN MORAL! REMAINING MORAL CAN BE ACHIEVED THROUGH GOOD COMPANY AND KEEPING YOUR MIND AND BODY INVOLVED IN GOOD, WHOLESOME ACTIVITIES!

There is a beauty every girl has--
A gift from God, as pure as the sunlight,
and as sacred as life.
It is a beauty all men love,
A virtue that wins all men's souls.
That beauty is chastity.
Chastity without skin beauty may enkindle the soul;
Skin beauty without chastity can kindle only the eye.
Chastity enshrined in the mold of true womanhood
will hold true love eternally. (David O. Mc Kay)

Let Virtue garnish thy thoughts unceasingly; then shall thy confidence wax strong in the presence of God; and the doctrine of the priesthood shall distill upon thy soul as the dews from heaven.

The Holy Ghost shall be thy constant companion, and thy scepter an unchanging scepter of righteousness and truth; and thy dominion shall be an everlasting dominion, and without compulsory means it shall flow unto thee forever and ever. (D&C 121:45-46)

Chapter 8

WHAT IS THE OPPOSITE SEX LOOKING FOR?

Both men and women are always wondering what the other feels or thinks about one subject or another. What is it that they like, what are they looking for? It is true that men and women do think differently about a lot of things, but it is also true that they think very much alike concerning most things. In addition, it should be noted that many differences between sexes do not conflict, but rather compliment each other. Therefore, if you are in a real stew about what the other sex thinks, you can often ask yourself how your own sex feels about it, and you won't be too far off in many cases. Both sexes seek pretty much the same type of qualities in their companion, and we have listed some of the most basic qualities below.

What are some "Loveable Qualities" that the opposite sex is looking for?

1. *Character:* Honest and ethical in dealing with others.
2. *Spiritual Dimensions:* Religious and moral.
3. *Industrious:* Ambitious, hard working.
4. *Intelligent:* Quick, educated and possesses good judgment.
5. *Social Maturity:* Makes friends easily and has a lot of friends. Congenial, a good mixer, has social poise and leadership.
6. *Good Family Orientation:* Comes from a good family and wants to be a good family person, a good parent.

7. *Good Temperament:* Stable and constant, dependable; not moody, but pleasant and cheerful to be around.
8. *Talented:* Skilled in many areas, handy with hands, maybe artistic or musically inclined.
9. *Healthy:* Strong and has good endurance, good at sports, no major illnesses and not often sick.
10. *Patriotic to Country:* Involved in the political process, willing to serve in community.
11. *Job Capacity:* Capable of making a good living and good at handling money.
12. *Romantic:* Remembers important dates, does little acts of kindness and gives of himself physically and emotionally.

The above qualities are sought by both men and women in their companions. Obviously no one has all of them, but we can work to develop as many of them as we can, and it will aid us in becoming more successful in our dating.

Through our questionnaires we compiled two lists of things that were suggested by both men and women as things they liked or didn't like in their dating companions. Many of them have already been listed above, but we will list them again:

UNDESIRABLE TRAITS

1. Dishonest and untruthful
2. Too egotistical and Boastful
3. Indecisive; can't make up mind
4. Too easily discouraged or depressed
5. Poor manners
6. Picks nose or teeth in public
7. (Girls) Uses too much make-up and puts it on in public
8. Poor manager of money
9. Too shy and introvertish
10. Pouts, sulks and is moody
11. Too aggressive and pushy
12. Stubborn and must have their own way
13. Criticizes partner in public
14. Flirts with others on date
15. Has body odors and bad breath
16. Uses profanity and tells bad stories
17. Uses poor English grammar
18. Uses alcohol, smokes, uses drugs
19. Overweight and sluggish
20. Argumentative and keeps bringing up past arguments
21. Shows off in driving a car
22. Too demanding and possessive
23. Wears rings on wedding finger

DESIRABLE TRAITS

1. Comes from a good family
2. Is considerate of parents and family
3. Controls temper
4. Has high ideals, moral standards etc.
5. Interested in cultural things--music, art, books etc.
6. Plans dates in advance
7. Organized in personal belongings
8. Positive & constant personality
9. Has a good sense of humour
10. Ambitious and hard worker
11. Likes children and wants family
12. Interested in sports
13. Neat in appearance, clothes, hair, shoes etc.
14. Compliments partner and shows appreciation
15. Remembers important dates, birthdays etc.
16. On time for dates and activities
17. Adaptable to situations, not too rigid
18. Encourages partner in major goals
19. Lives religion and stands by convictions
20. Does special romantic things occasionally

MORE THINGS TO LOOK FOR

There is something more important than realizing a few specific traits in a person, and that is knowing their most basic goals and the general orientation of their life. It may be helpful to realize that there are three basic kinds of people:

1. *PEOPLE ORIENTED:*
   They thrive on being around people all the time, they are very society conscious. They want to serve their fellow men constantly.
2. *THINGS ORIENTED:*
   They live for big cars, homes, boats, clothes etc. They spend their lives trying to find happiness in things.
3. *CONCEPT ORIENTED:*
   They live for learning, they love books and new experiences, they spend much of their lives working for degrees, studying and researching and love the challenge of intellectual exercises. They are committed to their philosophy or religious convictions.

Obviously people are not just one of these types completely, but they are a combination of all three, with greater emphasis toward one area. If a woman is very highly "Things Oriented," and she wants a lot of things that take loads of money, then she should be careful not to marry a person who doesn't care about "things" at all, and who isn't willing to devote his life to a specific area of research that doesn't pay very much. Likewise a very outgoing man who is "People Oriented" would need a woman who is also willing and hopefully interested in being around people much of the time. There are many situations that can evolve from different combinations of people's orientations.

Along with these orientation areas are some basic goals that divide people into other groupings similar to the above. The author has selected 6 *major goal areas:*

1. *Learning goals:* Goals of degrees and much learning.
2. *Religious goals:* Their religion means everything to them and their lives revolve around living their religion.
3. *Serving goals:* "People Oriented," they wish to spend a lot of their time serving in different positions and committees etc.
4. *Entertainment goals:* Some people live their lives with the whole goal of just relaxing, watching TV, entertaining themselves or traveling. Life is to enjoy things and to be entertained. They don't wish to allow other things to take too much of their time.
5. *Family goals:* Those who live for their companions and their children. Everything they do in their spare moments is for or with the family.
6. *Wealth and Power goals:* They want money and high positions.

Again, most individuals have a combination of many of these goals. Hopefully they are well-balanced, well-rounded and have a proper perspective of all of them. But usually people are dominated by one or two of these goals. This being the case they need to find a companion that is "looking for" the same things, and working for the same goals as they are!

RELIGIOUS GOALS

If our dominating goal is religious, and we desire to spend long hours of our life in church activities and wish to donate large amounts of money to a church; then we must have a companion that shares our goal or life will be lonely and conflicting much of the time. Religion is very emotionally loaded and is often quite demanding of our time. Religious goals and beliefs break up more marriages than divorce records show. Other reasons are given, but at the base of many marriage problems is a conflict in religious belief. A religious companion will often put religion first, and to the non-religious companion it seems that they are being excluded, whether it was meant that way or not.

One of the most important criteria that you can place on a marriage partner is to make certain that you share the same religious values. If you are not religious, then don't try to tie someone down to you that is religious. The Jewish person needs someone to take them to the Synagogue and the Catholic needs someone to take them to the Catholic church. Mormons are taught from childhood that they need to have someone who can take them to the Mormon Temple to be married. The Protestant faiths need at least another Protestant, and hopefully from the same denomination.

It is not only important to marry someone of the same faith, but someone who is our "spiritual equal," who feels and thinks with the same degree of devotion. It is not sufficient to marry someone who is of the same church in name only. When we marry a person with the same spiritual dimension and the same religious goals, then we greatly increase the chances that our marriage will be deeply fulfilling, peaceful and happy. Our joys will be multiplied from the harmony of our spiritual unity.

Some couples survive the conflicts of religious ideals for quite a while, but the real conflict arises when the children come and both parents are determined that the children will have the same religious upbringing that they had received. Yes, "A family that prays together stays together."

The same illustrations and conflicts can be shown for other conflicting "*goals.*" Your dating will be more successful if you analyze your own goals first, and then search for a companion with similar goals.

WHICH SEX IS SUPERIOR?

The battle between the sexes as to which sex is more important and which one is superior has gone on throughout the ages with no fitting conclusion. Those who engage in such arguments have little value for their own time. I think some of the writing of John Ruskin in *Sesame' and Lilies,* p. 155, has treated the subject very beautifully. He writes:

> *We are foolish, and without excuse foolish, in speaking of the "superiority" of one sex to the other, as if they could be compared in similar things. Each has what the other has not: each completes the other, and is completed by the*

> *other: they are in nothing alike, and the happiness and perfection of both depends on each asking and receiving from the other what the other only can give.*
>
> *Now their separate characters are briefly these. The man's power is active, progressive, defensive. He is eminently the doer, the creator, the discoverer, the defender. His intellect is for speculation and invention; his energy for adventure, for war, and for conquest, wherever war is just, wherever conquest necessary.*
>
> (Of the woman's position he says:) *Her great function is praise: she enters into no contest, but infallibly adjudges the crown of contest. By her office, and place, she is protected from all danger and temptation. The man, in his rough work in open world, must encounter all peril and trial: to him, therefore, the failure, the offense, the inevitable error: often he must be wounded, or subdued, often misled, and always hardened. But he guards the woman from all this; within his house....This is the true nature of the home: it is the place of peace; the shelter, not only from all injury, but from all terror, doubt and division. In so far as it is not this, it is not home; so far as the anxieties of the outer life penetrate into it, and the inconsistently-minded, unknown, unloved, or hostle society of the outer world is allowed by either husband or wife to cross the threshold it ceases to be home; it is then only a part of that outer world which you have roofed over, and lighted fire in. But so far as it is a sacred place, a vestal temple, a temple of the earth watched over by household gods.*
>
> (Of the woman he says:) *She must be enduringly, incorruptibly good; instinctively, infallibly wise--wise, not for self-development, but for self-renunciation: wise, not that she may set herself above her husband, but that she may never fail from his side.*

It seems to the author that the above illustrates the separation of roles between the man and woman quite well. If only it were as simple as the language of John Ruskin! It appears to the author that most of the deeper problems of marriage arise from the conflict of leadership.

WHO SHOULD BE THE DOMINANT LEADER?

Back to the initial question of the chapter, what is the other sex looking for? In most cases, women are looking for a man that they can look up to and desire to follow. And conversely, a man is looking for a lady that will admire him and allow him to take the lead.

The author went with one girl for some time and was having problems making real progress. One day her father took him aside and explained to him that his daughter wasn't any 19th century girl, and that she wouldn't be a puppet pulled by her husband's strings. With her it was going to be a 50-50 proposition in marriage. There are many that feel this way, that everything should be 50-50. Marriage certainly is a give and take situation, but the more the author has thought about the 50-50 proposition, the more he disagrees with the concept. It infers that half of the decisions will be made by one and the other half of the decisions by the other. "Let's see now, who made the last important decision?"

Most women do not want to make half of the decisions. It is not only uncomfortable for them, but it is unfulfilling for them and the man whom they wish to please. Some women are better at making decisions than men, but most of them aren't--not because they are inferior, but simply because it isn't their nature and role to develop the art. Even when they are good decision makers, they feel more comfortable letting the man take that traditional role.

Even when the man takes the dominant leadership position of making the major decisions, it doesn't mean that the woman won't still have plenty of decisions to make in her own area. She has her own personal items, and it is a rare husband who wants to decide what face cream his wife uses! She will usually make most of the decisions in purchasing food and small items for the home. There will be many areas that are left for her to decide upon. In addition to these decisions, she will usually share in the major decisions as well. Most men want to counsel with their wives and get a lot of feedback from them so that even major decisions are made jointly and in unity. However, when unity can't be obtained and a decision must be made--it should be the husband's role to make the final decision, with the wife conceding and giving her support to him--even when it becomes obvious later that it was a bad decision.

THE MOST WONDERFUL GIFT A MAN CAN EVER RECEIVE & THE MOST BEAUTIFUL GIFT A WOMAN CAN EVER GIVE: It isn't the CAVE MAN approach of the man taking the woman by the hair of the head and dragging her around as he pleases. It isn't a matter of women being abused and never getting their way. It is not a matter of a man taking these rights by physical force. If a man has to stand up and fight and argue for the dominant role on every turn, then in truth he really hasn't got it!

The beauty of the whole concept is that it is a GIFT from the woman. She allows and even encourages the man to take the dominant leadership position. She submits willingly and helps her man realize his potential. She gives up no free agency in so doing; she simply uses her agency to bestow the dominant role on the man. No matter which direction the man may go, they have both won. And the irony of it all is that women usually get more of what they want than if they had been up waving banners demanding equal rights. For as a man senses his wife's great love for him by taking a submissive role, he will in turn break his back to please her. It no longer becomes a matter of 50-50, but he will more likely make decisions which will give her 75 percent of her desires. He is more likely to make decisions with her interest at heart and his major goal will be to make her happy. It is indeed the most wonderful gift a man can ever receive and the most beautiful gift a woman can ever give; that is, giving the man the dominant role of leadership.

So much of the unhappiness in marriages develops simply because women won't give the gift, or the men won't take the gift. Many women want their men to take the lead, but the man insists that they do all of the deciding and take the lead in calling the shots in the family. Or, in a dating situation, it is common for a boy to insist that the girl pick the show, activity, or place to go for the evening. If you are the girl, you might tell the fellow in a friendly way: "I really don't like to make the decisions, you can please me best by making most of them. I'd rather that you suggest what you would like, and if I don't like it, I'll let you know. OK?'' Most fellows will be delighted.

And if you're a fellow and the girl is always making all the decisions before you get a chance to, you might say in the most pleasant manner you can: ''Look Sue, you're with me, and I kind of like to take the lead if you will let me, but you have to let me--I can't force you and still be any kind of a gentleman.'' Then the fellow needs to plan his dates ahead and let the girl know far enough in advance what he has in mind--so that she isn't ill at ease, wondering when some decisions are going to be made, or when they're going home etc.

EXPECTATION LEVELS: Fellows, you need to find out early in the date about any ''time pressures'' on the girl's part and assure her early in the date that you will have her home on time. Before leaving the home is the best time; then parents or roommates will have some awareness of the time you will return your date.

To further illustrate the need of defined expectation levels, the author will relate an experience he had. He had been going very steadily with one girl for some time. He had been seeing her nearly every night. Finally, a state occurred where she was always getting ''tired'' and seemed bored with his company. Then she started telling the author that it was about time to go home. This was OK for a while, but when it became a practice, he greatly disliked it. There was tension and unhappiness in the relationship. The author felt like telling her: ''Sure I'll go home, but don't look for me to come back.'' It was never at the same hour, he never knew what to expect. Finally the author got smart enough to realize that neither he nor the girl had a satisfactory understanding of each other's expectation level. So he came right out and told her: ''Look, I'm tired of you telling me to go home. Now, what time do you need to get up in the morning, and what time do you need to have me gone?'' They picked an hour and it solved the problem completely. She was less tired, there was less tension, and the writer felt less like an unwanted intruder.

You don't want to structure your relationship too much, but a little structure can do an awful lot to improve the relationship. If girls are starting to make many of the decisions, then it might be a clue for the fellow to realize that what they are really trying to say is: "I don't know where I stand, so I'll call the shots and then I'll know." So the fellows need to give the girls more of an expectation level that they can tentatively count on. It will help to relax them and make them feel more confident in your ability to take the lead.

In conclusion, then, we have talked about some of the qualities, traits, the orientation and goals that dominate different individuals. We have listed them in order to help you realize some of the things that the opposite sex is looking for. We have stressed the importance of religious goals. We have talked about the most wonderful gift a man can receive and the most beautiful gift a woman can ever give--in giving the man the dominant lead in a relationship. If you are a woman, then the opposite sex is looking for many qualities, but especially they dream of the glorious chance to lead and provide for you. If you are a man, then the opposite sex is looking for the kind of person they can look up to and respect enough to place their lives into your care and keeping.

Chapter 9

DEVELOPING A DATING PERSONALITY!

I. IT BEGINS BY ACCEPTING & BELIEVING IN YOURSELF!

Many times we are anxious to change the world and yield a dominant influence upon others when we haven't even learned to accept and believe in ourselves. Many people hate themselves, and if we could listen in to their thought waves we would discover a continuous line of self-depreciating statements. Large segments of our population are grossly unhappy and miserable simply because they have not established worthwhile "self-concepts." Throngs of people drag themselves through life feeling inferior to nearly everyone else around them. They are often threatened by the mere existence of others in their lives. They are fearful of venturing out of their caves of suspicion, worry and fear. Life is threatening and unrewarding to them.

In reality we all suffer from feelings of inadequacy at various times. We all have days and periods in our lives when we withdraw from society and shrink away into our caves. But most of us are willing to venture out into the light of the sun again and to keep trying. Failure is not a result of falling down, but the refusal to get up again. Success is not a destination, but an on-going journey. Accepting yourself, then, begins with the inward commitment that says with determination: *"I BELIEVE IN MYSELF AND I WILL ALWAYS KEEP TRYING, NO MATTER WHAT HAPPENS ALONG THE WAY!"*

To summarize the above we will list it as Key 1:
KEY 1: I WILL ACCEPT AND BELIEVE IN MYSELF!

II. CREATING AFFIRMATIONS:

The next step of accepting yourself begins by establishing a *DEFINITE SET OF GOALS* for yourself that you believe and know that you can achieve if you keep working at them. It is extremely helpful to physically write a list of your goals out on paper and to state them in the affirmative tense. They should be defined specifically and clearly. The following are some examples:

1. I will learn to play the piano well enough to play in a dance band!
2. I will graduate from College!
3. I will eventually find an excellent companion!
4. I will learn how to stand up in front of people and give a speech!
5. I will learn how to dance with above average skill!
6. I will learn how to bowl well enough to hit 180!
7. I will master the textbook of my history class well enough to obtain at least a B+!

These kinds of self-challenges are referred to as *AFFIRMATIONS.* It is extremely helpful to write these out and to carry them with you and read them over several times daily. You simply keep affirming them to yourself. It is important that you make them realistic and obtainable. It is also important that you plan an attack of intermediate steps which will help you obtain your specific "affirmations." We will now list the 2nd key in the form of an affirmation:
KEY 2: I WILL WRITE OUT AND WORK ON MY AFFIRMATIONS!

III. GATHER POSITIVE THOUGHTS:

The next step is to "gather thoughts!" To think about the goals you have, and gather in ideas that will help you to attain them over a period of time. Your thoughts must be mixed with some emotional drive and excitement in order for them to accomplish their desired goal. If you would like to read an excellent book that talks at length about these principles, the author highly recommends a book entitled: *Think and Grow Rich,* by Napoleon Hill. He states, "Thoughts which are mixed with any of the feelings of emotion constitute a magnetic force which attracts other similar or related thoughts." Your author likes to shorten that phrase to: *LIKE THOUGHTS GATHER LIKE THOUGHTS.*

The suggestions above are more powerful than you can presently realize until you have really worked with these concepts over a concentrated period of time. If you find yourself becoming depressed and discouraged, you can use the above concepts to turn off that magnetic force of negative thoughts quickly before the emotional density of the thoughts become strong enough to control your mind. Then using the same principles you can control and direct your mind to happy, positive thoughts. You can involve your emotions in gathering more and more right thoughts until you are thoroughly engrossed with progressive and productive activities. "The human mind is constantly attracting vibrations which harmonize with that which dominates the mind." Whatever the achievement you would like to obtain--whether it is a skill, a goal, wealth, or personal development--you can obtain it with the above formula. "Just concentrate on the objective at hand." Choose your affirmations and gather thoughts for their success.

The people who are unhappy with life are those who don't have positive projects going all the time that they are involved with and excited about. For your own mental health, peace and happiness--get several projects going. They may be found in the form of a hobby, a collection, developing a skill, learning a musical instrument, writing a poem, a story, or a book. It may be creating an invention, beautifying your home or personality. It may be building your own business and fortune on a part time basis or full time. Whatever your affirmations, remember, they are obtainable through your faith and belief in yourself.

DEVELOP A POSITIVE NATURE: Using the above concepts, you can work on developing a more positive personality. Speak in positive tones, greet yourself with a smile in the morning and when you speak to people--let them know what a great day it is. Let them know that you are happy and that you feel wonderful; let them know that you feel life has a great future. When people get angry at you, respond with understanding and return warmth. Minimize your discouragements and maximize your successes. Remember that thoughts are like sheep--they follow each other. Sheep have been known to follow each other over cliffs. Your thoughts are capable of being just as foolish unless you give them positive direction.

"As if" Theory: If you find you are unhappy and discouraged, then "act as if" you are happy. If you want to be more graceful, more dynamic, more accomplished, then "act as if" you are and you will find yourself becoming just that. You are becoming tomorrow what you think about today.

Light of the Body: In the Bible, Matthew 6:22-23 tells us: "The light of the body is the eye: if therefore thine eye be single, thy whole body shall be full of light. But if thine eye be evil, thy whole body shall be full of darkness. If therefore the light that is in thee be darkness, how great is that darkness!" As you allow your eyes to fasten on to evil scenes and thoughts, those types of things will begin to possess your body. But as you place your eyes and concentration on wholesome things, spiritual things, then your entire body will be consumed with those things. How much light radiates from your eyes?

Mind Inertia: The science of physics uses a term called "Inertia," which is defined: "A body at rest tends to remain at rest, and a body in movement tends to remain in movement." Thus it is hard to push a car to start with, and it is hard to stop a car once it is moving fast. Likewise, once your mind is placed in motion to think about negative things, bad things, immoral things, etc., it will tend to remain in motion in that direction. It will gather other thoughts of the same kind until you step in and turn your mind in a positive direction.

There are many ways of illustrating these dynamic concepts of controlling your mind, building a positive personality, and obtaining your desired affirmations, but we will sum it up with:

KEY 3: I WILL GATHER POSITIVE THOUGHTS CONSTANTLY!

IV. YOU ARE WEALTHY IF YOU HAVE A GOOD SMILE!

You can't get to first base in developing a positive personality unless you are willing to develop and use a few muscles in your face, specifically the ones that form a *smile.* Your smile is vital in convincing people that you are a positive person. A smile is inviting, it usually means that you are friendly and approachable. It relaxes a person and makes them feel you accept them. It communicates to those in a dating situation that you want to see more of them, that you may like them. If given with great depth it means I LOVE YOU! To salesmen it is worth millions, because a man with a smile is nearly always welcome.

A SMILE

Costs nothing--but gives much. It enriches those who receive, without making poorer those who give. It takes but a moment, but memory of it sometimes lasts forever. None is so rich or mighty that he can get along without it. And none so poor that he can be made rich with it. A smile creates happiness in the home, fosters good will in business, and is the countersign of friendship. It brings rest to the weary, cheer to the discouraged, sunshine to the sad, and is nature's best antidote for trouble. Yet it cannot be bought, begged, borrowed, or stolen, for it is something of no value until it is given away. Some people are too tired to give you a smile. Give them one of yours--as none needs a smile as much as he who has none to give.

KEY 4: I WILL DEVELOP A CONTAGIOUS SMILE!

V. KEEP BUSY LEARNING AND DOING THINGS:

What do you do if you're unhappy? What if you don't feel like smiling? Then it is time to use the "as if" theory; act "as if" and you will soon be. In the writing of *The Once and Future King,* by T. H. White, Merlyn was the magician and teacher to King Arthur. When asked what to do for being sad he replied: "The best thing for being sad, is to learn something! That is the only thing that never fails." That little message has so much power in it for those who will use it. There are few things more stimulating than discovering new things in a book or having someone teach you a great thought or help you to acquire a skill. It is stimulating and engrossing and best of all, it takes sadness away. Too many wait for happiness to reach out for them, and it just doesn't happen that way. We must do the reaching, and that is one of the reasons why we become happy--WE have done it! William James put it this way:

Action seems to follow feeling, but really action and feeling go together, and by regulating the action, which is under the more direct control of the will, we can indirectly regulate the feeling, which is not.

So the thing to do in curing sadness is to begin by smiling and then get yourself involved in doing things. Become anxiously engaged in a good cause. Become involved in good groups. Develop some worthwhile hobbies. Now let's read more of how Merlyn put it to King Arthur:

The best thing for being sad is to learn something. That is the only thing that never fails. You may grow old and

> *trembling in your anatomies, you may lie awake at night listening to the disorder of your veins, you may miss your only love, you may see the world about you devastated by evil lunatics, or know your honour trampled in the sewers of baser minds. There is only one thing for it then--to learn. Learn why the world wags and what wags it. That is the only thing which the mind can never exhaust, never alienate, never be tortured by, never fear or distrust, and never dream of regretting. Learning is the thing for you. Look at what a lot of things there are to learn.... You can learn astronomy in a lifetime, natural history in three, literature in six. And then, after you have exhausted a milliard lifetimes in biology and medicine and theocriticism and geography and history and economics--why, you can start to make a cartwheel out of the appropriate wood, or spend fifty years learning to begin to learn to beat your adversary at fencing. After that you can start again on mathematics, until it is time to learn to plough.*

Therefore we apply **KEY 5: I WILL KEEP MYSELF BUSY LEARNING AND DOING GOOD THINGS!**

VI. INTROSPECTION:

The process of introspection involves self-analysis. You look within and see where you can improve yourself. You ask yourself what you are doing right and wrong. Don't forget to look for the good points, because introspection can sometimes be destructive as we are often too hard on ourselves. Spend time looking for good qualities in others that you can emulate or take on yourself. Emulation can produce revolutionary changes for the good if you pick good people. This is the method by which we learn even as children, and we never cease learning from others. Beware of your models however; don't bestow upon them all perfection or you may some day be greatly disappointed. Differentiate between their positive traits and their whole person. You don't want to be entirely like them--you want to be yourself, with slight remodeling of certain traits.

Benjamin Franklin's approach: If you have read the autobiography of Franklin, you know that he ascended to the heights of his greatness by constantly working on some trait he wished to acquire. He would single out one trait and work on it for at least one full week, giving it all of his attention and doing everything in his power to control the successful use of the trait. Then he would proceed to another trait. Everyone should develop their own, but for the purpose of suggestion we will list the thirteen traits that he would repeatly work on: Temperance, Silence, Order, Resolution, Frugality, Industry, Sincerity, Justice, Moderation, Cleanliness, Tranquility, Chastity, and Humility.

In the early part of his life, Franklin wanted to improve his writing, so he read from those whom he considered to be great writers, then he would attempt to write in the same manner they had, checking himself periodically. This is an example of emulation mentioned above.

To aid the reader in improving his personality, the author has put together a couple of lists with which readers may rate themselves and pick out certain areas that they would like to work on to improve. First a Negative list, then a Positive list:

NEGATIVE TRAITS OF PERSONALITY

1. Do you interrupt people to interject your own opinions?
2. Do you correct people's statements rather regularly?
3. Do you speak negatively of other people behind their backs?
4. Do you cut down your leaders all the time and tell others how they should lead?
5. Do you have a tendency to take the opposite viewpoint for the sake of conversation?
6. Do you correct a person's speech or flaws in front of others?
7. Do you mimick the faults and flaws of others?
8. Do you have a tendency to be looking for the faults and flaws of others?
9. Do you try to be clever or show your sense of humour through sarcasm?
10. Do you tend to not look at people that are speaking to you?

11. Do you always think your suggestions are better than those presented?
12. Do you resent authoritative figures, those you have to work under?
13. Do you raise your voice in anger very often?
14. Do you throw others up as examples of what your friends should be?
15. Do you have a tendency to be discouraged with yourself and depreciate yourself?
16. Do you carry grudges for a long time, are you sulky and slow to forgive?
17. Do you become a poor sport when someone beats you at something?
18. Do you act impatient in waiting your turn?
19. Do you act blunt and curt in your pronouncements?
20. Do you act intolerant and cynical of others?

POSITIVE TRAITS OF PERSONALITY

1. You listen to others! You make sure you understand them by restating their ideas.
2. You usually agree with people and give supporting evidence to support their ideas.
3. You are quick to congratulate people for their latest achievements.
4. You are quick to defend a friend and bring out his good points.
5. You are observant of people's dress and grooming and compliment them.
6. You smile a lot.
7. You are anxiously engaged in good causes.
8. You have positive goals and ambitions.
9. You are energetic, enthusiastic and positive.
10. You radiate confidence and you are outgoing, people oriented.
11. You are able to disagree in a humble way; "I may be wrong, but I thought...."
12. You respond with positive answers when people ask you how you are.
13. You have a good sense of humour that is not cutting or personal.
14. You are a good listener when people need to talk.
15. You are anxious to learn new things and go out of your way to learn things.

16. You are more concerned with the comfort of others than your own.
17. You remember important dates, birthdays and special events.
18. You are on time for appointments.
19. You are dependable and follow through with commitments and agreements.
20. You are *honest.*

It may be a little difficult at first to rate yourself on these, because we are not usually completely bad in any one area, but neither are we completely without need of improving in the various areas. Put OK by those you feel you are good in and don't need to improve upon, put an "x" by those you are weak in, and a double "xx" by those that you are terrible in. If you have more than 50 percent x's, then you have considerable improving to do. If you didn't have any x's, then you didn't read number 20 very well!

KEY 6: I WILL USE INTROSPECTION AND CONCENTRATE ON MY WEAK TRAITS!

VII. DEVELOPING THE ART OF CONVERSATION!

Sooner or later everyone becomes tired of all the small talk that goes on in conversation. Those who have done a lot of dating, for example, must go through some of the same lines at every turn. If they dance with twenty different people at a stag dance, they are likely to hear some of the same remarks twenty times: "Where are you from, what are you doing, working or going to school? What is your major, what do you hope to do with it? Great weather isn't it?"

After a while you feel like a broken record and an insincere one at that. What can a person do to improve the conversation? The only answer there can be is to go beyond the generalized small talk into more *SPECIFIC* conversation about the person you are talking to! After you have given the "small talk" question of "Where are you from," then continue asking questions about the place they are from. After you have asked, "What is your major," then continue to ask specific questions about their major and what areas they enjoy the most. *EVOLVE FROM THE GENERALITIES TO THE SPECIFICS!*

Talk to their interests, and attempt to get them to start talking about them. Many people think that in order to be great conversationalists they need to be talking all the time, when just the opposite is true. You are not successful until you have brought the other person out of their shells and have them talking with great enthusiasm about the things they are excited about. So the secret is to find out what it is that they are interested in and excited about. Learning to be a *GREAT LISTENER* is paramount in being a great conversationalist.

Beware not to embarrass people and push them on a topic they seem to be reluctant to talk about. If they are famous or a great expert in something, they will often not want to talk much about it, simply because everyone does. In the event that you have trouble getting them to say much, you may need to take more of the lead. In doing so, *first* talk about the kinds of things that you think they might be interested in. *Second,* try to choose a topic which you are well acquainted with and of which you can talk with some degree of intelligence. *Third,* talk about everyday things going on in the world. The best conversationalists usually do a great deal of reading. Read the newspaper, listen to the news broadcast, read a news magazine and formulate some opinions about things going on around you, so that you can talk about them. One of the best magazines that you can get for conversation is the *Reader's Digest,* for it will give you the cream of the crop from all the other magazines. I challenge you to try reading it for a while and you will find it unbelievable how often you will spontaneously start talking about the things you have read in the *Reader's Digest.* As you do take these steps of keeping up on things by reading, deliberately practice talking about a few of your readings. The more you do it, the more you will find it comes naturally. Another idea is to observe others in conversation and observe what makes them successful.

KEY 7: I WILL DEVELOP THE PERSONALIZED ART OF CONVERSATION!

VIII. THE COMPLIMENT CLUB:

In talking about conversations, the very best way to get a conversation going is to give a good compliment! The world is starving for appreciation, for recognition, for praise, and the trouble is that we leave them hungry too often. We all need to spend more time recognizing each other in positive ways, to give people a moment of acceptance. If you would improve your personality, you must learn the art of praise, you must increase your compliments many, many fold, and you must completely do away with the use of criticism. You may still need to suggest and encourage and stimulate improvements and corrections, but you must do away with the crude, cutting direct criticism.

A famous psychologist named Dr. George W. Crane relates that while he was teaching Psychology classes one evening, a young girl had come to him complaining that she was lonely and without friends and felt that everyone else was snobbish and indifferent. So Dr. Crane assigned the class, the next time, to apply their psychology *BY GIVING COMPLIMENTS TO THREE DIFFERENT PEOPLE EACH DAY FOR THIRTY DAYS!* They were to be strangers and different people every day. The students had to be positive and "social detectives" in ferreting out good things about people. It created miracles for many of them! The girl that had been the cause of the assignment ended up getting engaged to one of the men in the class.

He had another girl come in on the verge of a nervous breakdown, and she blamed her boss, who was so rude and mean to her, but she didn't feel like she could give up the job. So Dr. Crane directed her to compliment her boss. She resisted greatly but finally found something she could compliment him on. Later she ended up marrying her boss!

If you want to be successful in the dating world, you must constantly find things to compliment and praise in those you are courting. If we want success with people in general we need to compliment and praise them, whether they are under us or over us. We ought to perfect our ability to compliment people to the point that we can even compliment our enemies and our most unlikely friends. Someone has said that we ought to love our enemies because we made them. And Abraham Lincoln said that "the best way to destroy your enemy is to make him your friend."

There are different ways of complimenting people; you can do it directly or indirectly. You can ask them for advice or ask them their opinion--that is a compliment. You can say nice things about them to others in front of them or even when they aren't there. You can compliment their family or their personal objects. Alexander Pope once said that the best way to compliment a man is to say something favorably about the things in which he is aspiring to be proficient, rather than the routine tasks or job in which he is obviously adept already. The author recalls a time when a man was chosen to replace him in a church calling. The author didn't know the man, but did know his outstanding wife. So before about 400 people he mentioned that he didn't know him, but if he had married his equal, he had to be very outstanding. He came up afterwards and said that it was the nicest compliment anyone had ever paid him.

Another aspect of compliments is to join what is called the League of the Golden Pen. Everyone becomes a member that accepts the challenge to write at least one note or letter per week and send it to somebody who merits condolence, sympathy or praise. You don't have to know them, and it can't be a regular letter you should be sending anyway.

The author hopes that you will accept many of these suggestions as a challenge to test them out, but especially you should accept this key and challenge:

KEY 8: I WILL CEASE TO CRITICIZE, BUT WILL COMPLIMENT AT LEAST THREE PEOPLE DAILY!

IX. SENSE OF HUMOUR:

How important is it that you have a sense of humour? It is vitally important! This doesn't mean however that you have to be the funniest individual around, nor does it mean that you have people rolling over with laughter all the time. But it does suggest that you need to be able to laugh and see the lighter side of life.

Healthy Personality: The difference between people who have emotional and mental problems and people who don't is often only a difference of how seriously they take their problems. There are many medical exceptions to this statement, but it is still very common. Everyone has problems, but it is how you handle them that counts. One of the greatest lessons we can learn is to not worry about the problems that we can't do anything about! Learn to get involved with other things, get emotionally excited about solving other kinds of problems that aren't of a personally threatening nature. Help others with their problems and you will soon forget your own. Someone has said that if we could tie all of our problems up in a bundle and have everyone throw their bundle in one big heap, and then give them the chance to select a new bundle--that people would rush to retreave their own!

What we need to do is laugh our problems away. We need to develop the art of not taking ourselves too seriously. When we make a mistake or experience some failures, we need to give some brief analysis to them in hopes of not repeating them again; but after we have given them a brief period of introspection, we must learn to drop them. Some problems we can just drop and forget, but others are too emotionally involved, and the only way we are going to get off the worry kick is to replace the worrying with something else--humour. Abraham Lincoln had a childhood sweetheart that he felt very deeply about, who died, and a short time after the death, Lincoln was in the company of others and was doing a lot of joking and laughing. Someone criticized him for laughing at a time like that, and he replied: "Don't you see, if I don't laugh I must cry." Many other people have found a little humour helpful when they are trying to forget unhappy thoughts.

Humour can be enjoyed when no one else is around, just by being able to enjoy yourself when things are not going well. You learn to see the lighter side of things. Too many try to be funny in front of others when they haven't practiced long enough by themselves. But practicing doesn't infer acting, for real humour is more of an attitude than an act. It is creative, in that you look beyond the surface appearances of things. You see things that others don't see and you are able to express them in a fun way.

Light-mindedness: Too many individuals confuse light-mindedness with good humour. They often appear closely related, but are really miles apart. A light-minded person involves individuals and uses them as the "goat" of their adulterated humour. If they aren't making fun of the individual directly, they make fun of things which are private, special or sacred to that individual. This is *not* humour--it is sacrilege to try and make laughter at the expense of other individuals. A sense of humour implies some "sense." Occasionally humour can involve individuals, but not to the point that they are made fun of or made to feel foolish, or goated in any way. Humour usually involves objects or situations.

The first step in developing a sense of humour is to possess the ability to *ENJOY OTHER PEOPLE,* to like people and to understand people, and the capacity to enjoy life with them. The second step in developing a sense of humour is the ability to enjoy yourself! Many people can't enjoy their own company, they hate themselves. If we are supposed to love our neighbor as ourselves, may the Lord protect some poor neighbors! Many of those who hate themselves and don't have self-accepting images, attempt to justify their position by saying that they need to stay "humble," and if they thought too much of themselves they wouldn't be humble. This type of humility is adulterated humility--it isn't true humility. The truly humble person really believes in himself and knows that he has something to offer the world. The real starting point of humility is self-acceptance.

True humility accepts the reality of believing that one is a "Child of God," and if therefore he knows that he is a child of God, he knows that he has "eternal potentialities!" He knows further that God loves him and that he would be untrue to God as well as to himself if he did not believe in himself. Humility can only accept truth and gravitates toward the lofty, the ideal, the good, and there is none of this in self-pity and self-degradation. It has been said that God must have a sense of humour or he wouldn't have created some of us. Hopefully, we too can develop some humour for our lives.

KEY 9: I WILL DEVELOP A MEANINGFUL SENSE OF HUMOUR.

X. DEVELOP A RELAXED COMPOSURE:

Part of the art of successful conversation has to do with the ability to relax and show some composure. It is vital to your success with people to radiate an air of confidence, a certain poise. Not rigid or stiff, not too formal, but a certain coolness that stimulates the confidence of others in them. They seem to know what to do, how to do it, and when to do it; people with composure know how to handle a situation. They display a magnetism that shows they are happy and accepting of themselves and others.

It is easy to talk about sometimes, but it often seems that when we want to impress someone, we become tongue-tied and feel that we are very awkward. How does one overcome this nervousness? The following are a few suggestions that may help:

1. *Lower the pitch* of your voice. When we are nervous we have a tendency to speak at a much higher pitch than is normal to us. The high pitch betrays our nervousness even more.

2. *Slow your speech down.* This will give you more control and will also aid in lowering the pitch as just mentioned.

3. *Get the other person talking,* and this will let you off the hook more until you can feel more relaxed. Ask questions that take sentences or more to answer.

4. When you must talk, *talk about things you know something about* and can talk about with confidence.

5. *Relax your muscles by breathing* in a little more air, but don't make it too noticeable. Suggest a walk when it is possible. This is relaxing sometimes.

KEY 10: I WILL RELAX AND DEVELOP COMPOSURE!

XI. DEVELOP A GENUINE LOVE FOR OTHERS:

The Christian ethic has proven itself over and over as the real antidote for unhappiness. Two main principles, paraphrased from Matt. 7:12 and Mark 12:31, are:

1. *DO UNTO OTHERS AS YOU WOULD HAVE THEM DO UNTO YOU.*
2. *LOVE YOUR NEIGHBOR AS YOURSELF.*

If the world would follow these two principles with true discipleship, our problems of war, strife, and unhappiness would be over. The social problems of the world would take care of themselves. Individual problems would also change, because we would soon lose ourselves in serving others. Their problems would take the place of our own and we would soon forget our own little reasons for being unhappy. We would be caught up in making other people realize that we understand them and accept them with all their fears, their anxieties, and their weaknesses.

EMPATHY: This is the word used to describe the above ability to appreciate another person's problems as if they were our own. Our ability to empathize with others will in large measure determine our ability to "RELATE" to them in a deeper and more significant manner. True empathy goes beyond just understanding. It implies that we are willing to do something about our feelings. It implies that we are willing to spend time with a person and get ourself involved in their life and help them work out their problems just like we would if they were our very own problems. We would then truly lose ourselves in SERVING our fellow men. We have then made significant achievements in the area of "loving our neighbor as ourself."

ARGUMENTS: Every relationship with other human beings has its moments when there are disagreements. At these times we are most anxious to stick up for our rights and to set the other person straight with our brilliant set of words and reasoning. But later on the words we used are not remembered, only the consideration and love we displayed, or the lack of it.

> *The words are only as snowflakes that soon melt. They are like feathers that are quilted into a feather-down bed; once they are quilted away, no one remembers from where they came or how they looked upon the feathered bird. All that is known is the feeling and comfort they provide for us now.*

So we must have the perception to look into the future and speak with soft words and with understanding words even when we feel we have been wronged. Henry Ford said that "if there is any one secret of success, it lies in the ability to get the other person's point of view and see things from his angle as well as from your own."

Once we are certain that we have a total understanding of their position and still feel certain that we need to correct them, then we must still do it with love and understanding. We must use extreme tactfulness in order to retain their friendship. One definition of tact helps illustrate this idea. "Tact is the ability to tell someone to go to hell (Hades) in such a way that he is looking forward to the trip." But remember that the justification to criticize is next to nonexistent. "There is so much good in the worst of us and so much bad in the best of us, that it doesn't behoove any of us to criticize the rest of us."

To summarize this section then, if we would be happy, if we would bring happiness to others, we must develop the ability to use "empathy" and to relate to others. We must learn the ability to understand their position as clearly as we would our own if we are to be successful in following key 11.

KEY 11: I WILL DEVELOP A GENUINE LOVE FOR OTHERS!

XII. REALIZE THAT THERE IS A SPIRITUAL DIMENSION TO ALL MEN!

We may develop ourselves in all the other areas and still remain losers until we learn to respect those things which are sacred to all men. Maybe their philosophy or religious beliefs seem strange to us, but we must recognize that it is nonetheless very sacred to them. Those who would be successful must learn to be understanding and tolerant of the beliefs of others.

In addition to developing a tolerance, a successful person must weigh their own beliefs and convictions and live up to them. There is little to a person's personality when there is no character, no values, no honesty and no direction. We must develop direction to our lives, and seek out religious beliefs! If we cannot maintain any specific belief, at least we should develop our own code of religious values. We must realize that there is more to life than just the body. There is a "spirit" within the body that needs nourishment as well, and it is fed through righteous living, good living and by meditating upon spiritual or religious thoughts. We have already listed the second great commandment to love our neighbor as ourselves, but we must not forget the first commandment: *TO LOVE THE LORD OUR GOD!* This body of clay will eventually be laid down, but the spirit and "*Developed personality*" will continue to exist for the eternities.

KEY 12: I WILL DEVELOP SPIRITUAL VALUES!

Before we relist the 12 keys that we have developed in this chapter, the author felt it might be interesting to consider some lists created by others. There are many helpful thoughts in them that we have not had the space to cover. First he will give the list prepared by Napoleon Hill; and then Dale Carnegie. Your author would highly recommend that you read their books! Especially Carnegie's: *How to Win Friends & Influence People,* and Hill's: *Think and Grow Rich!*

THIRTY FACTORS OF A PLEASING PERSONALITY

1. A positive Mental Attitude
2. Flexibility of Mind
3. Sincerity of Purpose

4. Promptness of Decision
5. Common Courtesy
6. Pleasing Tone of Voice
7. The Habit of Smiling
8. Tactfulness
9. Facial Expression
10. Tolerance
11. Frankness in Manner & Speech
12. A Keen Sense of Humour
13. Faith in Infinite Intelligence
14. A Keen Sense of Justice
15. Appropriateness of Words
16. Control of the Emotions
17. Alertness of Interest
18. Effective Speech
19. Versatility
20. Fondness for People
21. Control of Temper
22. Hope and Ambition
23. Temperance
24. Patience
25. Humility of the Heart
26. Appropriateness of Clothing
27. Good Showmanship
28. Clean Sportsmanship
29. Ability to Shake Hands Gracefully
30. Personal Magnetism

SUMMARY OF DALE CARNEGIE'S— HOW TO WIN FRIENDS & INFLUENCE PEOPLE

(Your author's words)

Rules: To Make People Like You:

1. Show genuine interest in others.
2. Smile!
3. Remember names.
4. Learn to listen.
5. Talk in terms of their interests.
6. Make other persons feel important.

Rules: To Win People to Your Way of Thinking!

1. Avoid all arguments.
2. Respect opinions, never tell them they're wrong.
3. If you are wrong--admit it quickly!
4. Begin in a friendly way.
5. Get person saying "yes."
6. Let them do a lot of the talking.
7. Let them feel it was their idea.
8. Perceive their point of view.
9. Sympathize with their ideas and desires.
10. Appeal to nobler motives.
11. Dramatize ideas.
12. Give them a challenge.

Rules: To Changing People!

1. Give praise and appreciation first.
2. Point out mistakes indirectly.
3. Admit mistakes of your own before listing theirs.
4. Suggest by questions instead of ordering.
5. Help them save face.
6. Praise smallest improvements.
7. Assume their future success.
8. Make errors appear easy to correct.
9. Make them happy about following your suggestions.

Rules: For Home Life (Also Usable in Courtship!!)

1. Don't nag!
2. Don't try to make your partner over.
3. Don't criticize!
4. Give honest appreciation.
5. Pay little attentions.
6. Be courteous!

Now in conclusion, we will repeat the 12 KEYS of this chapter and hope they will be helpful to you! The author challenges the reader to improve upon these affirmations, to change or alter them to suit your own purposes. Add to them more specific kinds of things that you have hopes and desires of obtaining. Write them out and read them often, repeat or affirm them in your mind until you have established an emotional drive to see them fulfilled.

SUMMARY TO THIS CHAPTER—DEVELOPING A DATING PERSONALITY:

12 KEYS STATED AS AFFIRMATIONS:

1. *I will accept and believe in myself.*
2. *I will write out and work on my affirmations.*
3. *I will gather positive thoughts constantly.*
4. *I will develop a contagious smile.*
5. *I will keep myself busy learning and doing good things.*
6. *I will use introspection and concentrate on my weak traits.*
7. *I will develop the personalized art of conversation.*
8. *I will cease to criticize and will compliment at least three people daily.*
9. *I will develop a meaningful sense of humour.*
10. *I will relax and develop composure.*
11. *I will develop a genuine love for others.*
12. *I will develop spiritual values.*

The author has written this book for the purpose of making the dating world an easier place to be, and a more enjoyable place. It is understood that you probably will not agree with every word, but it is sincerely hoped that it has helped the reader in some small ways. Authors very seldom hear from their readers, but because of the nature of this book, this author would greatly appreciate some feedback. If you have learned anything that you feel may have helped you, would you specify which idea it was and from which chapter. The author would delight in hearing of your experiences in relationship to using the concepts of this writing. If it is OK to use your experiences in later publications, please give your permission. Names may be left out if desired. Please address your letters in the following manner:

HAWKES PUBLICATIONS
Editorial Dept. (D.B.)
Box 15711
Salt Lake City, Utah 84115

—APPENDIX—

In the writing of this book, the author created many questionnaires, some of them were given out to just groups of girls, others were designed and given out to just groups of fellows. Then there were others designed and given out to young married couples to see what they might say. The main concepts and ideas have already been brought out in the chapters of this book, but there has been considerable interest in the actual questions and how they were answered. Not all of the questions are listed here. Out of the hundreds of questions asked, only a few were selected that seemed to be the most interesting and which provided worth while information for daters.

SPECIAL QUESTIONS GIVEN TO THE GIRLS:

1. What kind of dates do you prefer for the first date? Which kind do you dislike the most for the first date?

Answer: There were a great variety mentioned for both. Movies had the highest rating for the most preferred date, but it also had the highest rating for the most unpreferred date. Many girls also mentioned swimming as an undesired date.

2. What percentage of the dating would you prefer to be double dating if you had your choice?

The large majority answered between 30 to 50%.

3. How far in advance do you think a fellow should ask you for the average week-day date?

11% answered 1 day; 19% = 2 days; 31% = 3 days; 6% = 4 days; 3% = 5 days; 11% = 7 days.

4. How far in advance do you think a fellow should ask you for a week-end date?

0% = 1 day; 6% = 2 days; 11% = 3 days; 19% = 4 days; 8% = 5 days; 44% = 7 days.

The above were the days they preferred; but those below are those mentioned as being ok:

31% = 1 day; 25% = 2 days; 25% = 3 days; 3% = 4 days; 3% = 5 days; 11% = 7 days.

5. Often a fellow wishes he had made a date, and even though you prefer more notice than a few hours, would you usually still be pleased to have him call you? Yes 90%

6. Do you enjoy being lined up with a fellow's friend? Yes 64%
Do you enjoy being lined up by your own friends? Yes 64%

7. Does it bother you if a fellow you are dating doesn't have a car?
Yes 19%

8. Does the niceness of his car have much influence in impressing you? Yes 5%

9. If you don't think a fellow is going to make much money in life, does it weaken your interest in him? Yes 22%

10. At what stages of feeling do you permit a fellow to kiss you?

a. I feel it is only proper to let a fellow kiss me after he has dated me a few times, whether I have any feelings for him or not?
Yes 8%

b. I often like a fellow to kiss me to see if I feel anything for him? Yes 8%

c. I would only let him kiss me if I had at least a little feeling for him? Yes 42%

d. I would let him kiss me only if I knew I liked him a great deal? Yes 39%

e. I would let him kiss me only if we were going steady, etc.
Yes 3%

11. Out of the fellows you have dated three or more times, what percentage would you guess have kissed you?

5% of the time = 3%; 10% of the time = 6%; 50% of the time = 22%; 70% of the time = 8%; 80% of the time = 8%; 90% of the time = 8%; 100% of the time = 11%.

(The reason for some of the higher answers were qualified by statements such as: "I don't date them three times unless I am really excited about them, thus the chances for them kissing me is greatly increased.")

12. Assuming that you like each other, as a general rule, how many dates would you prefer before a fellow attempted to kiss you?

Number of dates: 1 date = 17%; 2 dates = 21%; 3 dates = 33%; 4 dates = 8%; 5 dates = 16%; 6 dates = 6%.

13. Would you like a fellow to ask you for permission to kiss you or just kiss you?

100% said to just kiss them and don't ask!

14. If a boy wants to kiss you, where would you prefer that he did the kissing?

a. Out on the date when you are alone some time. 22%
b. In the car on the date somewhere. 3%
c. In the car just before he takes you in. 28%
d. At the door before he takes you in. 47%

15. How long would you generally think you would like to know a fellow before you progressed into the following stages of commitment?

a. Going steady. (Most of them indicated about 2 months.)
b. Becoming pinned. (Between 2 to 4 months.)
c. Becoming engaged. (Most of them were around 6 months.)

16. List a couple of the dating activities that you thought were the most fun?

The most frequent answers were: Canyon parties, picnics, sporting activities, dancing and hiking in that order.

17. If a fellow calls and you are busy, how many alternate times should he suggest before hanging up?

Most of the answers were either one or two times.

18. If a fellow calls you and you are busy, how many more times should he call back before he should give up?

The majority of the answers were two or three times.

19. Do you like a fellow to give you alot of say in the dating activity, what show to see, etc?

Nearly all of them stated that they wanted to be told what do do and for the fellow to take the lead, at least for the first period of dating.

20. Have you ever lied to a fellow to get out of dating him and not hurting his feelings? Yes 72%

21. Do you feel the fellow must appear to be as intelligent or more intelligent before you could be interested in him?

75% said they had to be either as intelligent or more.

22. What little mannerisms bothers you most in fellows?

Feminity, indecisvieness, nervousness, talks too much, loud, rude, brags, and talks about other girls.

23. On the first date, do you think a fellow should offer his arm while walking?

Nearly all answered yes, especially on stairs and streets.

24. What do you think of a fellow who takes your hand on the first date, while walking or sitting?

88% thought it was alright while walking and 60% thought it was alright while sitting. Some girls were fearful of their own hands perspiring.

25. Would you prefer after the first date getting asked for the second date before you go in, or would you prefer that he called you later on the phone?

75% preferred to be asked before going in.

26. Do you think it is fun to have a fellow just drop in on you once in a while without notice?

70% answered yes, while the others were very much against the idea.

27. What do you think of a fellow dating room mates?

Only 20% thought it was ok.

28. Some fellows feel it is their role to tease a girl some, do you like to be teased as long as it isn't over done and not too personal?

93% Yes

29. What do you think when a fellow wants to go to a drive-in show on the first date? 69% Against idea.

30. Do you wonder sometimes if you have passed up marrying someone that you should have? 17% Yes

31. Are there times when you wish badly that you had a date and wish you could just call a dating service on the phone and get a date?
    50% Yes

32. Do you think that you could marry a fellow that you weren't physically attracted to a great deal?
    34% Yes

SPECIAL QUESTIONS GIVEN TO THE FELLOWS:

1. Do you wish girls would be more aggressive in making their acquaintance with you? 63% Yes

2. If you had been trying unsuccessfully to date a girl, how would you feel if she called you on the phone and talked a few minutes to you? 87% in favor.

3. How would you feel about a girl that called you that you hadn't made any advances toward? 54% against.

4. How much notice do you usually give a girl for a date during the week?
    Answers ranged from 1-7 days, but mostly 1-2 days notice.

5. In percentages, put down a guess of how you think your dating pattern would break down into these three areas:
    (a) ____% of the time I call a girl I just want a date and some company to relax with.
    (b) ____% of the time I call a girl I need a date for specific thing I want to go to.
    (c) ____% of the time I call a girl I am calling because I specifically want a date with the girl I am calling.
    Answers varied, but the averages were about: a. 10%; b. 20%; c. 70%.

6. What do you usually take a girl to on the first date?
    Just about everything was mentioned, but a show was highest.

7. About what percentage of your dating is double dating? 25%

8. Would you do more double dating if you knew someone to go with? 60% Yes

9. About how many times have you tried to kiss a girl on the first date?

51% said never; 49% said that they had, but not very often.

10. If a girl turns your kiss down the first time, would you usually stop dating her? 17% Yes

11. For what reasons do you often kiss a girl?

(a) Do you ever kiss a girl as kind of an experiment to see how you feel about her? 25% Yes

(b) Do you ever kiss a girl just for the pleasure of it? 79% Yes

(c) Do you feel that your relationship has to have alot of promise before you would kiss a girl? 56% Yes

(d) Do you save your kisses for just the one that means the most to you at the time, or would you kiss more than one in the same week if you felt so inclined?

45% indicated that they would kiss just one girl at a time.

(e) Would you rather not kiss a rather steady girl friend if you knew she was probably loving up some other guy on an alternate night? 77% Yes--rather not kiss her.

12. When you try and kiss a girl for the first time, where do you usually try to do it?

(a) During the date, but not in the car. 4%

(b) In the car on the date. 17%

(c) In the car just before you take her in. 34%

(d) At the door step just before you take her in. 45%

13. After how many dates do you think that girls rather expect to be kissed?

The range was from 1-10 dates, but the majority were 3 dates.

14. Which styles of hair do you prefer on a girl, long or short?

65% preferred long to short, but many didn't care.

15. Do you feel sometimes that girls rather expect to be teased once in a while? 81% Yes

16. Do you ever just drop in on a girl without notice? 49% Yes

17. Do you ever call a girl Friday or Saturday night and ask for a date on that very night? 53% Yes (Knew the girl usually.)

18. When a girl keeps telling you she is "busy" how many times all total will you usually call before giving up?

Most of the answers were between 2 and 3 times.

19. How many times would you guess you have dated in the last year?

The range was greatly varied, but a large number of fellows indicated that they had had at least 100 dates, many with same girl.

20. How many different girls have you dated in the last year?

The range was from 1 to 50, but mostly around 10 girls.

21. Do you like to have buddies line you up once in a while?

78% Yes

22. Do you like to have a girl line you up once in a while?

65% Yes (They seem to prefer fellows to line them up.)

23. Do you feel that your real happiness can not begin until you are married? 37% Yes

24. Do you ever go up to a girl that doesn't know your name and ask her for a date? Yes 43%

25. Do you ever wonder if you might have passed up someone that you should have married? 46% Yes

26. Are there alot of girls you would really like to date, but don't seem to have the courage to ask them? 38% Yes

27. Which do you fear the most, (a) getting hurt by a girl, or (b) hurting them?

a. 39% getting hurt; b. 61% hurting them.

28. Being honest, have you ever had a girl hurt you? 94% Yes

29. Do you ever find yourself dreaming about some girl you had a crush on a long time ago that isn't even around any more? 68% Yes

1. What do you think the biggest problem is that old maids and bachelors need to overcome to get themselves married?

Answers varied, but the most frequent were: too selfish and demanding, want someone that is perfect, and not willing to accept faults in others.

2. Do you think that some of the older unmarrieds should just decide that within the next three months they are going to pick the best thing they can find and try to get married?

11% Yes with conditions; 89% definite No.

3. Many claim that it was hard to feel right about the person they became engaged to at first, did you? 41% Yes

4. Many claim that they had strong doubts during the engagement and just before the marriage, did you? 40% Yes

5. Many claim that they went into marriage with some doubts, did you? 26% Yes

6. Have you had many doubts as to it being the right thing since marriage? 21% Yes

7. After how many dates did you first kiss the one you married?

Nearly 50% kissed their companion on the first 2 dates.

8. How long did you date the person before you knew they were the right person?

Answers had great variation from 1 date to years, but about half of those questioned were under three months.

9. How long did you date the person before you became engaged?

The average seemed to be about six months.

10. How long did you date the person before you became married?

Ranged from 2 months to five years; but average was about 17 months.

11. Are you one of many that feel that you could have married several other people and been just about as happy? 35% Yes

12. Estimate about how many different persons you dated in your life? (1 to 300; but not counting highest numbers, it appeared that the average was about 24.)

13. How many of these did you go real steadily with?
The average was about 3.

14. How many of these did you propose to or received a proposal for marriage?
Average was 2.3 people.

15. Knowing what you know now, how long do you think an engagement should be?
There were two main groups of answers, those who felt it should be under 6 months, and those that felt it should be over 6 months to a year.

16. So many unmarried people look upon marriage as the thing that will solve their problems of unhappiness, and if they could just get married they would then be happy! What do you think of this idea?
All were against idea, they indicated that marriage was "no panacea," and that marriage increased the probability of problems.

17. Do you think that a person should be more concerned with the parents of their partner than they usually are?
73% Yes (Singles rated this question with little importance.)

18. Are you sorry that you kissed others as much as you did before marriage? 87% No

19. Do you think there is anything to the idea of trying to save your kisses for just your marriage partner? 73% No

20. Are there some important things that you think a couple should talk about before they are married?
There were many answers, but nearly 80% of them included money! Over 60% of them mentioned sex. Some of the other frequent answers were: in-laws, number of children, education, etc.

21. Do you think there is any wisdom in putting off having children a little while?

65% Yes

22. Do you ever find yourself still thinking once in a while about another person that you liked at one time?

60% Yes

23. Some say that romantic crushes over others still come and go after marriage and you just have to close your mind to them; have you found this to be true at all?

43% Yes

24. There are many who fear before marriage whether they will be sexually satisfied or if they will satisfy their partner; are these fears realistic?

About 65% said Yes! Those who indicated Yes, felt that there should be some discussion on the sexual hopes or expectations of the other before marriage.

25. Do you think that alot of fellows and girls kill relationships by one of them letting the other know that they like them too soon?

54% Yes

26. Give the approximate ages when you were married?

Averages: wifes--20.2 years; husbands--22.3 years.

The author felt it was interesting to ask these questions to the young married's and that much was learned from it. However many of the questions that are frequently asked by "single's" were not understood. This was evident by the types of answers they gave or by the fact they wrote that they didn't understand the question. This was further evidence to the author that those who are married, even the young married's, can not fully appreciate the position or questions of single people.